FOREWORD BY NORVEL HAYES

THE VOICE OF ONE CRYING

OF ONE

A Prophetic Message For Today!

JOHN BEVERE

DOVE PRAYERLINE, INC.
P. O. Box 7375
Alexandria, LA. 71306
Ph. (318) 445-5453

The Voice of One Crying:
A Prophetic Message for Today!
by John Bevere

Copyright © 1993 by John P. Bevere

ISBN 0-9633176-1-X
Printed in the United States of America

Library of Congress Catalog Card Number: 93-091567

Published by John P. Bevere
John Bevere Ministries, Inc.
P.O. Box 2002
Apopka, Florida 32704-2002

Direct inquiries and/or orders to the above address.

Cover art by Doug Belew/Belew Design, Tulsa, Oklahoma.
Photo by Dennis Rosenquist.

CONTENTS

Foreword   v

Introduction   1

Chapter 1   The Elijah Anointing   5

Chapter 2   The Prophetic Ministry   15

Chapter 3   The Voice of One Crying   29

Chapter 4   Prepare the Way of the Lord   39

Chapter 5   Wolves in Sheep's Clothing   55

Chapter 6   Depart from Me: I Never Knew You   65

Chapter 7   True or False Repentance?   79

Chapter 8   The Gospel of Self   95

Chapter 9   Flee from Idolatry   109

Chapter 10   Good Root—Good Fruit   121

ACKNOWLEDGMENTS

My deepest appreciation to . . .

All those who labored with us in prayer, in project, and by financial support to bring this book to completion; to our ministry staff for their constant support and faithfulness; to Amy, Angela, and Doug for their many talents.

I want to thank my wife, Lisa, who selflessly helped with editing, but more important, for the godly wife she has been to me. I love you, darling!

A special thanks to my three sons, Addison, Austin, and Alexander, who sacrificed time with Daddy so that this project could be completed. You boys are special gifts from heaven above!

Most important, my sincere gratitude to our Father in Heaven for His indescribable gift, to our Lord Jesus for His grace and truth, and to the Holy Spirit for His faithful guidance during this project.

FOREWORD

The most important thing in the world is salvation. Without it you're not going to heaven, and without repentance there is no salvation. *The Voice of One Crying* is an excellent book on the subject of repentance. I challenge everyone who reads this book to yield to the cleansing of the heart and soul through repentance. We can no longer live by the world's standards. God has called us to a holy life. Only through repentance can we hope to attain the kind of cleansing that gives us right standing with the Father, that we may have eternal life.

I strongly urge leaders and laymen alike to speak up with love and authority. Stop tickling ears and begin to lead the church into repentance so that we may be found spotless, blameless, and without wrinkle upon the return of our Lord Jesus Christ.

As you read this book, look at your personal relationship with God. Let it speak to you. Don't look at your neighbor and start judging him; God wants to speak to *you*.

God is seeking to raise up men who will do and say what is necessary to keep the church on course. John Bevere is one of those men. I've known John for ten years and have found him to have a pure heart, boldness of character, and a relationship with God which is evidenced by his stability.

Dr. Norvel Hayes
Author / Teacher
Norvel Hayes Ministries
Cleveland, Tennessee

INTRODUCTION

This book is a message to the Church. It is also for those who have left the church structure due to discontent or offense. It is a message for Christians of any denomination or membership—or those who want nothing to do with denominations or memberships. It is for those in the full-time ministry as well as those not in full-time ministry. It is a book for young and old, whether they've known the Lord for many years or have just come to serve him recently.

As we are poised on the brink of a new millennium, there are questions facing all of us. Are we in revival? Are we experiencing the outpouring of God's Spirit and the harvest of souls that the prophet Joel foretold? How do we compare to the Church in the book of Acts? Are we the glorified Church Jesus is coming back for? Are we ready for His return?

Is it possible we have accepted hype and emotional excitement as a poor substitute for revival in the last few decades? Have we become a people who love appearance and not substance, thereby producing no depth?

Have we forsaken godliness and integrity for what many call "advancing the kingdom"? Is the world seeing Jesus Christ in us by our genuine love for one another? Is what we have exemplified in the '80s and '90s our destiny?

The forthcoming revival that Joel prophesied will be different from what many are expecting. It will not be through a church system that reeks of the world. It will not come through a lukewarm, idol-worshipping Church nor by ministries competing and striving with one another. It will not come as long as we compromise integrity for success. The world will not be attracted by the glamour and glitter of the Church, but will rather be drawn by its glory.

The cause of this present-day lapse in the Church is due to the life-styles we've lived and preached in the latter part of the twentieth century. We have reduced the gospel to a cheap solution to life's problems. We have sold Jesus like salesmen trying to meet their sales quotas! In doing this we have by-passed repentance to get a *convert*. So *converts* we have. The question is, what kind of *converts* do we have? Jesus said to the ministers of His day, "You travel over land and sea to win a single *convert*, and when he becomes one, you make him twice as much a son of hell as you are" (Matthew 23:15, NIV). Converts are easy to make, but are they truly sons of the kingdom of God?

This book addresses all these issues as well as many more. In the fall of 1992 the Spirit of God commissioned me to write this book. As I wrote, I trembled with awe, for what God was giving me was much stronger than what I had thought. In fact, at one point I stopped writing. I did not want to say some things quite as strong as they came to me. After several weeks had gone by, I started writing again, trying to change the way I had said some things. I was getting nowhere. It seemed the anointing to write was gone. I spent hours at the computer trying to write, but the flow of the Spirit was not there. I began to pray and seek the Lord concerning this book. I said, "Lord, If You want me to write this book, you are going to have to give me the words. It seems that nothing is flowing, and there is no life and anointing in this." The Lord spoke back to me quite clearly and said, "You strayed six weeks ago from what I desired; return to where the life and anointing was once flowing." I went back to that chapter where I had left off and immediately the anointing to write returned. I then continued nonstop until this book was complete.

I have preached much of what is written in this book across the United States and overseas. However, a good portion of this book came to me as I wrote. I had never heard it, preached it or thought of it before. This was another confirmation that this book was inspired of the Lord. I know this message is the cry of God's heart to His people in these last days. Please do not take it lightly! I want to encourage you to read this book in its entirety; the message would not be complete if you read only part of it. As you read this book ask the Lord to apply it to your life that His way may be prepared in your life and ministry. The Church will be transformed as each individual member of the body changes. Too often we think everyone else must change, and not ourselves. Much of what I have written concerns areas that God has dealt with me about personally in preparing me for these last days.

The Lord is indeed returning for a holy and glorious Church, not having spot or wrinkle or any such thing (Ephesians 5:27). We must keep this vision before us that we do not become discouraged and lose what has been promised. When God calls us to repentance, it is for us to be changed and to move into the hope that is set before us. John the Baptist's message was, "Repent, for the kingdom of heaven is at hand!" (Matthew 3:2). In other words, he was proclaiming, "The kingdom is at hand, so in order to receive what God has for you there must be change (repentance)." **To preach repentance without hope will lead people into legalism.** We must change in order to come to the place that we can receive what God has promised.

This message is a message of mercy from the heart of God, not judgment. Mercy, because He is warning us that He is coming in His glory whether we as individuals are ready or not. So in order to receive what He has for us we must change what is presently not of His ways so that when His glory is revealed we may be glad with exceeding joy!

My prayer is that as you read this book you will hear God's voice in it to you, that your ears may hear and your eyes may see and your heart may recognize and understand what the Spirit of God is saying to you and the Church in these last days. I also pray that He reveal Himself and His will to you through this book so that you may be ready for what He has called you to in these last days.

1 THE ELIJAH ANOINTING

God's judgment will be according to His righteous standard, not our own.

> Behold, I will send you **Elijah the prophet** before the coming of the great and dreadful day of the Lord. And he will turn the hearts of the fathers to the children, and the hearts of the children to their fathers, lest I come and strike the earth with a curse.
>
> Malachi 4:5-6

THE DAY OF THE LORD

The great and dreadful day of the Lord—the second coming of Christ—may be closer than you or I think. God says that He is going to send Elijah the prophet before the coming of that day. It will be a **great** day for the *faithful* and *wise servants* of the Lord and a **dreadful** day for those who never received the gospel of Christ and those who have were *unwise* and *wicked servants* of the Lord. These are the ones who, though they knew His

5

will, did not do it! This is illustrated in the following words of Jesus:

> And the Lord said, "Who then is that **faithful and wise steward**, whom his master will make ruler over his household, to give them their portion of food in due season? Blessed is that servant whom his master will find so doing when he comes. Truly, I say to you that he will make him ruler over all that he has. But if that **servant** says in his heart, 'My master is delaying his coming,' and begins to beat the male and female servants, and to eat and drink and be drunk, the master of that servant will come on a day when he is not looking for him, and at an hour when he is not aware, and will cut him in two and appoint him his portion with the **unbelievers**. And that **servant who knew his master's will**, and did not prepare himself or do according to his will, shall be beaten with many stripes. But he who did not know, yet committed things deserving of stripes, shall be beaten with few. For everyone to whom much is given, from him much will be required; and to whom much has been committed, of him they will ask the more" (Luke 12:42-48).

The great and dreadful day of the Lord is His return to execute judgment. God's judgment will be according to His righteous standard, not our own. On this day, "The loftiness of man shall be bowed down, and the haughtiness of men shall be brought low; the Lord alone will be exalted in that day, but the idols He shall utterly abolish" (Isaiah 2:17-18). It is the day of vengeance on the pride and disobedience of man, even though now it seems as if haughtiness and rebellion go unnoticed, unpunished, and often rewarded.

Many today are deceived. They live for themselves but believe they are right with God. Their hardened hearts have lost the fear of God. Of these we are told ". . . that scoffers will come in the last days, walking according to their own lusts [desires], and saying, 'Where is the promise of His coming? For since the fathers fell asleep, **all things continue as they were** from the beginning of creation'" (2 Peter 3:3-4). These men and women walk according to their self-seeking desires, not God's. Some deeds are even done in the name of Christianity. Their standard is not Jesus; they compare themselves with each other. The acceptance of society is their standard. Their reasoning goes something like this: "Why should I live a holy life-style when many in the Church don't live that way and they go unpunished? In fact, they even seem to prosper in what they do. Why should I put an unnecessary burden on myself?"

The Lord will rise in judgment by saying, **"I have held My peace a long time, I have been still and restrained Myself.** Now I will cry like a woman in labor, I will pant and gasp at once. I will lay waste the mountains and hills . . ." (Isaiah 42:14-15). God has been still and restrained Himself for a long time. The purpose of this delay is salvation. Many will turn and return to the Lord in this season, while others will grow harder and harder as they refuse His call. To them the day of the Lord will come unexpectedly.

"For you yourselves know perfectly
that the day of the Lord so comes as a
thief in the night. For when they say,
'Peace and safety!' then **sudden destruction**
comes upon them, as labor pains upon a
pregnant woman. And they shall not
escape" (1 Thessalonians 5:2-3).

The day of the Lord shall come as it did in the days of
Lot. Sodom and Gomorrah were fruitful cities with no
lack of food or shelter. There was no sign of impending
judgment. Everything was the same as it had been for
their fathers. "They ate, they drank, they bought, they
sold, they planted, they built . . ." (Luke 17:28). They
were caught totally unaware. They must have thought
God took no notice of the condition of their hearts and
the perverseness of their ways.

Lot was even unaware of the coming judgment. Lot
could represent fleshly, carnal Christians. We see this
by where he chose to dwell (among the inhabitants of
Sodom and Gomorrah), the type of wife he had, and
the children he fathered by incest, the Moabites and
Ammonites. By contrast, Abram chose to live a separated life. He was looking for the city whose builder
and maker is God. Lot chose to take fellowship with
the ungodly rather than live a separated life. The ways
of the ungodly slowly but surely began to bear fruit in
him and his family. No longer were his standards dictated by God; they were dictated by the society around
him. Lot became ". . . oppressed by the filthy conduct
of the wicked (for that righteous man, dwelling among
them, tormented his righteous soul from day to day by
seeing and hearing their lawless deeds)" (2 Peter 2:7-
8). The day of judgment would have come on him as a

thief in the night also, had it not been for the messengers God sent to warn him. However, even with this warning of judgment, his wife chose to look back because she had been so influenced by the world that she no longer feared the Lord. That is why Jesus warned us by saying, "**Remember Lot's wife.** Whoever seeks to save his life will lose it, and whoever loses his life will preserve it" (Luke 17:32).

ELIJAH COMES FIRST

God said He would send Elijah the prophet before the great and dreadful day of the Lord. This Elijah who is to come is not the Elijah of 1 and 2 Kings reincarnated. The text is not referring to a historic man, nor is it limited to a mere man. Rather, it describes the true meaning of "Elijah." To explain, the word Elijah comes from two Hebrew words: *el* and *Yahh*, *el* meaning "strength or might" and *Yahh* being the proper name for the one true God Jehovah. By putting them together we come up with "strength or might of Jehovah, the one true God." So what Malachi was saying was that, prior to the day of the Lord, God would send a prophetic mantle or anointing in the strength and might of the one true God.

Prior to Jesus' first coming the angel Gabriel appeared to Zacharias, the father of John the Baptist, and described the call upon his son's life as follows:

"And he will turn many of the children of Israel to the Lord their God. He will also go before Him in **the spirit and power of Elijah,** 'to turn the hearts of the fathers to the chil-

dren,' and the disobedient to the wisdom of
the just, **to make ready a people prepared for the
Lord**" (Luke 1:16-17).

John was the Elijah prophet sent to prepare the way of
the Lord prior to Jesus' first coming. He was "**the voice of
one crying** in the wilderness: 'Prepare the way of the Lord;
make His paths straight'" (Mark 1:3). The thrust of His
ministry was to turn the hearts of the children of Israel
back to God; his message: "Repent for the kingdom of
heaven is at hand" (Matthew 3:2). Repentance means a
change of heart, not just a change of action. The children
of Israel's actions were very religious, but their hearts were
far from God. Thousands attended synagogue faithfully,
unaware of the true condition of their hearts. So God
raised up the prophet John to expose their actual heart
condition. John declared to the multitudes, "Offspring of
vipers! Who warned you to flee from the wrath [**judgment**]
to come? Therefore bear fruits worthy of repentance, and
do not begin to say to yourselves, 'We have Abraham as
our father . . .'" (Luke 3:7-8, RSV).

He exposed the deception in which their hearts were
trusting. They believed they were justified because they
were children of Abraham and because of their faithful
attendance of synagogue and payment of tithes. John
was not sent to the heathen who had never professed to
know God; he was sent to awaken the "lost sheep" of the
house of Israel, to prepare them to receive Jesus.

John the Baptist fulfilled the Elijah prophecies for his
day prior to the Lord's first coming. However, Malachi
prophesied that this anointing would be sent prior to the
great and dreadful day of the Lord. This means there are
two different fulfillments of the prophecy. This is
explained in Matthew 17.

> Now after six days Jesus took Peter, James, and John his brother, led them up on a high mountain by themselves; and He was transfigured before them. **His face shone like the sun, and His clothes became as white as the light.** And behold, Moses and Elijah appeared to them, talking with Him (Matthew 17:1-2).

It is significant that Jesus face shone like the sun, and His clothes became white as the light, and Moses and Elijah appeared and talked with Him. For when Jesus returns on that great and dreadful day, He will rule and reign for a thousand years on the earth in His glorified body, and His saints will rule with Him. Continuing on, we read:

> Now as they came down from the mountain, Jesus commanded them, saying, "Tell the vision to no one until the Son of Man is risen from the dead." And His disciples asked Him, saying, "Why then do the scribes say that Elijah must come first?" Jesus answered and said to them, "Indeed, **Elijah is coming first** and will restore all things. But I say to you that **Elijah has come already,** and they did not know him but did to him whatever they wished. Likewise the Son of Man is also about to suffer at their hands." Then the disciples understood that He spoke to them of **John the Baptist** (Matthew 17:9-13).

Jesus spoke this after John was beheaded. Notice He

refers to two different time periods of the Elijah anointing: future (**is coming**) and past (**has come**).

Prior to the second coming of Jesus Christ, once again God will raise a prophetic anointing. However, this time the mantle will not rest upon a single man but corporately on a group of prophets and anointed men and women in the body of Christ. In the book of Acts, Peter quoted the prophet Joel:

> ". . . Your sons and your daughters shall prophesy . . . and on My menservants and on My maidservants I will pour out My Spirit in those days; and they shall prophesy . . . **before the coming of the great and awesome day of the LORD**" (Acts 2:17-20).

One of the definitions of the Greek word for "prophesy" in the above verse is to speak forth under divine inspiration. As we can see, this anointing to speak forth what God is saying will not be limited to just the prophetic office but will come upon pastors, teachers, evangelists, and apostles. It will come on those ministers who will follow God fully and who are not out to build their own ministries and are not intimidated by the opinions of men or organizations. This anointing will also come upon the remnant of men and women who will follow God wholly without the fear of man. Young men and women who are not in full-time ministry will flow in this anointing because it will come on the remnant of people in the Church who have not bowed their knees to compromise, thus preparing the Church for the return of the Lord.

Like John the Baptist, these Elijah prophets will go

after the lost or deceived sheep in the church structure, as well as those who have left through the "door of offense." There are many who attend church and feel they are ready for Jesus to return. Like the people of John the Baptist's time, they believe that by their works, good behavior, church attendance, tithes, or the fact that they once prayed the sinner's prayer, they are justified. They may believe they are justified, but the truth is they're not ready for His return.

There are ministers who live below the standard God has set for them. Their private lives are filled with the pursuit of gain and pleasure. They use the ministry to serve themselves and their goals. Some live as hypocrites; they ignore or terrorize their families while all the while acting spiritual and loving in the church. A leader cannot rise above where he is personally. He may appear to for a season, but sooner or later it will catch up with him. Not unlike the religious leaders of John's time, they believe that through their service, training, experiences, and good standing with fellow ministers and organizations they stand righteous in the eyes of God. Or they may believe that because many follow their ministry, God also approves of them. The Pharisees had a large following until the word of the Lord came to John in the wilderness and the multitudes left. Then these hypocritical ministers and came out to hear what God was saying through a man who not only yielded his mouth to God but also his entire life!

Yes, the day of the Lord will come upon the ministers who are lofty and proud. As a matter of fact, it will begin with them. There will be a sifting of their private lives and motives. They too have thought, "Ever since the fathers fell asleep, all things remain the same." Ministers of the Lord, bare your hearts now that you may fulfill

His call on your life and thus remove yourself from under His judgment.

Before you proceed to the next chapter, I urge you to read the Introduction if you have not already done so. The message of this book is strong. But it is strong to save lives, not to destroy them. It is strong to save ministers, not to destroy them. It may even remove the parts of your ministry that were built by the strength of the flesh. But remember: God does not destroy, root out, or tear down in our lives or ministries without building and planting what is new and fresh in its place. The message of this book is a message of His love and mercy. He warns us so we will not be judged with the world as Lot's wife!

2 THE PROPHETIC MINISTRY

If I want something from you, . . . you can manipulate, control, or dominate me.

> In those days John the Baptist came **preaching** in the **wilderness** of Judea, and saying, **"Repent,** for the kingdom of heaven is at hand!" For this is he who was spoken of by the prophet Isaiah, saying: **"The voice of one crying in the wilderness: 'Prepare the way of the LORD; make His paths straight.'"**
>
> Matthew 3:1-3

THE PROPHETIC ANOINTING

John was a preacher, not a teacher. To be more specific, he was a proclaimer of what God was saying. You do not find John the Baptist teaching anywhere in the Scriptures. This is characteristic of those who will walk in this last-days Elijah anointing. When they are operating under this anointing, they will primarily be proclaiming what God is saying. You will not find these men and women bringing forth a five-point sermon. To prophesy means to speak forth under divine inspiration. Another way of saying it is to be a "spokesman." God said to Moses concerning Aaron, "Now you [Moses] shall speak to him [Aaron] and **put the words in his mouth** . . . so he shall be **your spokesman** to the people. And he himself shall be as a **mouth for you**, and you shall be to him **as God**" (Exodus 4:15-16). The Lord said that Aaron would speak exactly what Moses told him to speak. Aaron would not be speaking what Moses had **said**, but what Moses was **saying. He would be Moses' mouth.** Later God said it this way, "See, I have made you **as God to Pharaoh**, and Aaron your brother **shall be your prophet**" (Exodus 7:1). Moses was the one with the message, but Aaron was the one to deliver it. So Aaron was Moses' prophet or spokesman.

Teaching establishes what has already been proclaimed. We will always have teachers in the body of Christ to strengthen line upon line what has already been preached. To prophesy, however, means to speak as the oracles of God. You don't go with a planned-out message. You open your mouth, God puts His words in, and you speak. You become God's mouthpiece!

Today, we have many people who teach the written Word of God. They speak to men about God. However, the Lord is raising up men and women who will not lean unto their own understanding and speak by the letter only, but will open their mouths and speak by the Spirit of God. If they teach, it will be prophetically, by divine inspiration, and not through a planned-out message from which they cannot deviate.

Much of what these prophets proclaim will call for change, for their primary mission will be to turn the hearts of the people back to God. Their messages may not seem "nice," but will deliver strong conviction. Their preaching will hit some areas like a hammer smashing a rock. They're going to command, rebuke, correct, and exhort with all authority, yet they will operate out of a heart filled with the love of God for His people. They will not be critical, suspicious, and judgmental as many self-appointed prophets are today.

There are many today who think that in order for a minister to be a prophet he must give prophecies, words of knowledge, and words of wisdom the way the people are accustomed to hearing them. A prophet may walk into a service and never say one "Thus saith the Lord . . . ." However, his entire message can be prophecy, words of wisdom, and words of knowledge! The reason most people would not recognize the prophet is because they are looking for his messages to be packaged the "usual" way, such as his messages prefaced with statements like "Thus saith the Lord . . . ."

John the Baptist never said, "Thus saith the Lord . . . ." In fact, most people in the Church today would have said that John the Baptist was an evangelist, not a prophet, because of the fact that many repented as a result of his messages and that he did not give personal prophecies. If we limit the prophetic office to what we think it is, because of what people have taught us in the past, we may miss what God is bringing in these last days through His Elijah prophets!

Some may say at this point, "But new testament prophecy is for edification, exhortation, and comfort." That is exactly what John the Baptist's ministry was for. Let's take a look at what He preached. Read carefully what he prophesied, and notice carefully the last verse.

Then he said to the multitudes that came out to be baptized by him, "Brood

of vipers! Who warned you to flee from
the wrath to come? Therefore bear fruits
worthy of repentance, and do not begin to
say to yourselves, 'We have Abraham as
our father.' For I say to you that God is
able to raise up children to Abraham from
these stones. And even now the ax is laid
to the root of the trees. Therefore every
tree which does not bear good fruit is cut
down and thrown into the fire . . . I indeed
baptize you with water; but One mightier
than I is coming, whose sandal strap I am
not worthy to loose. He will baptize you
with the Holy Spirit and fire. His winnow-
ing fan is in His hand, and He will thor-
oughly clean out His threshing floor, and
gather the wheat into His barn; but the
chaff He will burn with unquenchable
fire." **And with many other exhortations he
preached to the people** (Luke 3:7-18).

God called John the Baptist's preaching **exhortation!**
Yet he begins his message by calling them a brood of
vipers and then warning them that if they do not
repent they will be judged! Do you think we have had
a warped or limited view of what edification, exhortation, and comfort are? They are the truth that makes
you free.

If you need further confirmation, look at Jesus' messages to the seven churches in the book of Revelation,
chapters 2 and 3! To one Church He said that if they did
not repent He would *vomit them out of His mouth!* How
many today would consider that statement to be edification, exhortation, or comfort?

If you look at the way Jesus started each message to the seven churches, you will find that He said, "To the **angel** of the Church of . . . ." The Greek word for "angel" is *aggelos*, its definition is "messenger." This is the same Greek word used in describing John the Baptist's ministry in Mark 1:2: "As it is written in the Prophets: 'Behold, I send **My messenger** before Your face, Who will prepare Your way before You.'" "Messenger" here is the Greek word *aggelos*. These messengers sent to the churches in Revelation are the Elijah prophets; they are not bringing a nice teaching but are bringing the Lord's message of repentance to His Church.

One point that should be made clear is that one who prophesies in this day and hour will always speak in line with what has already been written in the Bible. For God has said that no one is to add to or take away from the words of the Bible.

THE TRAINING GROUND

Next notice where John was preaching: the wilderness. The training ground for these prophets will be the desert or dry places. Luke 1:80 says, "So the child grew and became **strong in spirit**, and was in the **deserts** till the day of his manifestation to Israel." John the Baptist grew and became **strong in spirit** in the wilderness! Not in the palaces, not in the seminaries, not in Bible school, not in the synagogues, but in the desert. Prophetically that should tell us that the training for this Elijah ministry is not easy! God is tough with them. It is like training for the Green Berets. They have to go through a much tougher training than regular boot camp soldiers. Why? Because

they're going to go into places that are much more dangerous than what those boot camp soldiers will ever face.
In the wilderness John learned that the Lord was his
source, not man or institutions. He was not supported
by the denominational headquarters or by his church.
He did not seek support from his mailing list or by any
wealthy businessmen. Nor did he seek support by sending out promise letters of God's blessings to men and
women who gave to his ministry. His motive was not to
get—it was to give.

He did not generate support by writing letters to local
synagogues, asking them to come and preach, then fill-
ing his schedule with the large synagogues every week so
his budget could be met. His needs were not met by
speaking smooth words to the wealthy and giving them
preferential treatment. His needs were met by the Lord!

John the Baptist learned that God was his total source
in that desert! No man or ministry sustained him.
Therefore, he was able to speak what God was saying
without the fear of being rejected! Too many preachers
today are bound by the concern of what their people
think of them or their messages. Their boards control
them, not the Spirit of God. The fear of being rejected
dominates them. So they are like puppets at the end of a
string, controlled by the approval of man.

Let me put it this way. If I want something from
you—whether it is your money, friendship, approval,
acceptance, a position you can offer me, or security
you can give me—then you can manipulate, control, or
dominate me. If I want anything from you, then you
become a source, and if I offend the source, then what
I want may get cut off. This is called the fear of man.
You cannot fear man and God at the same time. You
will fear one or the other. The reason so many minis-

ters have no unction (life) in their teaching or preaching is because they are bound by the fear of man! Psalm 111:10 says, "The **fear of the LORD** is the beginning of wisdom . . ." and Proverbs 29:25 says, "**The fear of man** brings a snare . . . ." If a minister fears God, he will operate in the wisdom of God. There will be liberty and life in all that he says and does. If a minister fears man, it will be a snare to him. A snare is a trap that men use to catch animals in. I asked the Lord one morning what the fear of man was. He said, "The fear of man is the fear of being rejected by man, without considering My rejection!" The fear of being rejected by man is a trap! Oh, how many Christians are bound by that trap of desiring man's approval. John the Baptist learned in the desert that God was his source. He wanted **nothing** from the people, and if people or leaders rejected him and the message God was bringing forth through him, it did not affect him, but rather them, because he needed nothing from them.

John learned to hear the voice of the Lord in the desert. He was not repeating what he heard another man teach. He didn't read books to get sermons. He didn't study for hours to get a new message. He wasn't instructed on how to prepare a sermon or trained in homiletics. He had an anointing from the Holy One. He sought God, and the Lord revealed Himself to John! He knew that God had said, "And you will seek Me and find Me, when you search for Me with all your heart" (Jeremiah 29:13).

One of my responsibilities when working in the ministry of helps for four and a half years was to take care of the ministers who would come to our church. I served at a large church in Dallas, Texas, and it was a multifaceted ministry. Many times these ministers would give me advice for the ministry to which they could see I was called. One man told me to buy a book on how to win friends and influence people. Another told me to get a book on dressing for success. He said that in the ministry you must always dress right. He instructed me to wear power ties and dark suits and never to wear short-sleeve shirts. Another said, "Always be at the right place at the right time. Go to churches and seminars where lots of pastors are and have lots of business cards with you. Let pastors know that you are available to come preach." Another said, "Always say positive things to your audiences; don't speak negatively to them." I'm sure many other young men and women have heard the same things in seminary or Bible school.

I guess these men didn't consider the ministry of John the Baptist. "Always be at the right place at the right time." There he was ten miles out in the middle of nowhere. He didn't advertise in the Christian newspaper about the prophetic seminar he was having in the desert. He didn't run ads in a Christian magazine, saying, "Come to my prophets conference, and you will be a prophet in one week." I don't even think he plastered flyers all over Jerusalem, announcing his convention. Yet the Bible clearly states that the Word of the Lord came to him in the desert. "Then Jerusalem, all Judea, and all the region around the Jordan went out to him" (Matthew 3:5). What or who brought all those people out to the desert?

How about this: "Always say positive things to your audience." The first words out of John the Baptist's mouth in Luke's Gospel were, "Brood of vipers!" That's how he opened the service! Can you imagine looking at the multitudes and telling them they were a bunch of snakes! How to win friends and influence people by John the Baptist!

"Dress for success!" He wore a $1,500, double-breasted, Italian-cut, camel-hair suit, with genuine lizard skin shoes, right? No, he probably had a piece of camel skin wrapped around him with a leather belt holding it together. He probably had dirty feet and bad breath. When he preached he may have accidentally spit on those who got too close, and his fervor was at a high pitch.

That is why Jesus said of him, "What did you go out into the wilderness to see? A reed shaken by the wind? But what did you go out to see? A man clothed in soft garments? Indeed, those who wear soft clothing are in kings' houses. But what did you go out to see? **A prophet?** Yes, I say to you, and more than a prophet. For this is he of whom it is written: 'Behold, I send My messenger before Your face, Who will prepare Your way before You'" (Matthew 11:7-10).

Hungry people will travel for miles and sit under uncomfortable circumstances to hear the Word of the Lord. Many in America are fed up with lifeless preaching and teaching. They are tired of hearing men speak without the unction of the Spirit. They are fed up with sermons that don't pierce the hearts and bring forth changed lives.

I was preaching in a church in California recently. I was to begin ministering on Sunday evening. I came early to hear the pastor preach Sunday morning, and it was wonderful. There was such life in it. I knew he had a message prepared, but he was not bound to it. I could tell the Spirit of God was speaking right through him even though he was more of a teacher than a preacher. He was teaching prophetically. He was speaking the oracles of God. The next day as I was in prayer, I asked the Lord why all pastors can't speak with that kind of unc-

tion and life. I was feeling sorry for the pastor who could
not speak as well as that man could. The Lord replied to
me by saying, "John, every one of the persons I have
called to minister can speak with that kind of life. The
only problem is that they limit Me by their preplanned
sermons and notes. They can't trust Me to speak
through them!" Men have limited God to their understanding of Him instead of allowing Him to operate
through them as a vessel. Every time I've yielded and let
God speak through me, He has revealed to me more of
His nature.

Why must we try to put God in the box of our mental
comfort zone? Too many try to put Him within their
intellectual limits. You cannot confine the move of the
Spirit to your understanding. To try to put God in your
realm of mental reasoning is like trying to hold the wind
in a cage. He is like the wind. To confine Him is impossible. All you can do is just yield to Him!

This nation needs men and women of God who will
not tickle the ears of the people to whom they are
preaching. We need ministers who will tell the people
what they need to hear, not what the people want to
hear! Men and women who know that God is their
source, not the churches or the people. In America
today, many ministers have learned how to punch the
right buttons to get the response they want. If their true
motive was revealed, it is that they want the people to be
excited about their own ministries so they will give big-
ger offerings and come back with their friends.

In many churches you will not hear a confrontational
message that would convict the members of their sin.
The condition of the Church grows worse and worse
because of ministers who are more concerned about
their reputations than proclaiming truth. We must

become as the Master, who "made Himself of no reputation" (Philippians 2:7). We need preachers who know that if God has to bring their provisions by way of ravens or angels, He can do it. He is not bound by the members of the church or the mailing list!

JOHN WASN'T LOOKING FOR A PLACE TO PREACH

John the Baptist did not train for the ministry as the other young religious men of his day. They all went to Bible school in Jerusalem and studied under Gamaliel to become priests, Pharisees, and teachers of the law. John's father was a priest—a high priest at one time. John's inheritance was to become a priest, as was his father. He too was to go to the school in Jerusalem and study, graduate, and become ordained. He would have then been placed in a synagogue for ministry. However, the more John sought the Lord as a young man, the more he was steered away from professional ministry. God, instead of leading him to seminary, led him to the desert!

Can you imagine the conflict that arose in him as his mind began to reason by saying, "All my friends that I've grown up with are going to Bible school. They will get diplomas and be recognized as leaders. They will be ordained and have the ability to preach in every synagogue in the country. What will they think of me? How will I ever fulfill this call on my life if I don't go to the conventions and pass out my business cards to all the pastors and tell them I can come preach in their synagogues? My fee for speaking will be less than most; I don't have a family to support. I am filled with the Spirit, and I know there is a call on my life to preach. My dad told me an angel announced my birth and ministry. If I go to the wilderness, no one will know who I am! I'll never get invited to preach!" However, the burning call to go to the wilderness won out over the screaming of his intellect. He decided to follow the Spirit no matter what family or friends thought, or no matter what tradition called for.

We read in Luke 3:2, "While Annas and Caiaphas were high priests, the word of God came to John the son of Zacharias **in the wilderness.**" Then Jerusalem, all Judea, and all the region around the Jordan **went out to him** (Matthew 3:5). John was not looking for a place to preach because "a man's gift makes room for him . . ." (Proverbs 18:16). He knew that God would open the doors of utterance to proclaim the Word that He had put in him.

I was the young adults pastor at a very large church in Orlando, Florida, from 1987 to 1989. The pastor of that church knew that God wanted to send my wife and me on the road full-time. So he came into a pastors' meeting at the beginning of 1989 and announced it. The pastor and I felt that the right time would be January 1, 1990. Based on that, the church kept us on salary till December 31,1989, and we were launched in January of 1990 as planned.

Now the end of November came, and I knew our salary was about to be cut off in one month and all I had booked was a meeting in a small church in South Carolina the first week of January and another church in Tennessee the end of February. All we had was three hundred dollars in savings, and I had two small children with needs to care for. My pastor, who is very well known in this nation, had given me a tremendous letter of recommendation and had made available to me a stack of six hundred address cards of churches to which he had been. I had made copies of the letter and was in the middle of addressing the envelopes to send out to those six hundred pastors when the Spirit of the Lord came on me and said, "What are you doing, John?" I responded, "I'm letting pastors know I am available to minister." He quickly said, "You'll get out of My will!" I said, "God, nobody knows me out there!" Then He responded by saying, "I know you!" I knew He was showing me that His way was not to advertise myself. Now I didn't call it advertisement, but that is exactly what it is! When I heard Him say that, I threw away those letters and envelopes that were addressed. This did not line up with what I was told in training for the ministry, but I knew God had spoken to me.

Since then we have not lacked one cent or been idle. We have not made one phone call or written one letter unless it was reported that a pastor wanted us to contact him. We have seen God open doors in ways that caused us to marvel. In the next two years we ministered in churches in seventeen states and five other nations.

Ministries in America have become political and professional in many ways. God is looking for men and women who will trust Him for their every need and not try to give Him assistance in doing it.

Today we have traveling ministries who send out promotional packages trying to sell their ministries to pastors. They call churches and prostitute themselves and their gifts. We have hirelings who travel and charge fees to "minister." They justify prostituting the gift of God by the reasoning that they have a budget to meet and churches don't always realize what their needs are. They will only go to a church and "preach" if they are guaranteed so much money and provision. They have made the churches their source and not God!

On the other hand, we have some pastors today who will give the traveling minister a portion of the offering while keeping much of it for "expenses of the meeting." They have become so stingy that they have forgotten that a man does not go to war at his own expense (1 Corinthians 9:7). They are so concerned about their needs not being met that they rob from the traveling minister. It all comes down to looking out for themselves. The love of God does not do that; it gives, while not seeking its own!

Both have caused the focus of ministry to become selfish. Money becomes the motivating factor. This is why wealthy people control many ministers. This is the reason we see these manipulating rich people seated in the reserved seats of churches and given a voice in leadership rather than godly men and women.

We must turn from our "ministry" ways back to God's ways. This is the purpose for which God is raising up this Elijah ministry in the latter days prior to His return. These men and women will be sent to the leadership and the rest of the Church to call them to repentance. They will ". . . go before Him in the spirit and power of Elijah, '**to turn the hearts of the fathers [church leaders as well as natural fathers] to the children,**' and the disobedient to the wisdom of the just, to make ready a people prepared for the Lord" (Luke 1:17).

3 THE VOICE OF ONE CRYING

Your fruit will reveal your call.

The beginning of the gospel of Jesus Christ,
the Son of God. As it is written in the
Prophets: "Behold, I send My messenger
before Your face, Who will prepare Your
way before You. **The voice of one crying** in
the wilderness: 'Prepare the way of the
LORD; make His paths straight.'"

Mark 1:1-3

THE BEGINNING OF THE GOSPEL
OF JESUS CHRIST

There are many who would say that John was an
Old Testament prophet and his ministry does not
apply to us today. If that was the case, why didn't God
inspire a fortieth book in the Old Testament and call it
"John the Baptist"? Instead He clearly describes the
ministry of John the Baptist as "the beginning of the
gospel of Jesus Christ" (Mark 1:1). He is found at the

beginning of all four Gospels. Jesus made this absolutely clear by saying in Luke 16:16, "The law and the prophets **were until John.**" And again in Matthew 11:12-13 He said, "And from the days of John the Baptist until now the kingdom of heaven suffers violence, and the violent take it by force. **For all the prophets and the law prophesied until John.**"

John's message was a message of repentance. Mark 1:4 says, "John came baptizing in the wilderness and **preaching a baptism of repentance.**" The word "baptism" means to immerse or overwhelm. His message was not a partial repentance to enter the kingdom of God but a total repentance of heart. There are many today who are preaching that men and women can be saved by simply praying a sinner's prayer and joining themselves to a church. This often produces a counterfeit conversion, for when the people asked Peter what they needed to do to be saved, he boldly stated, "**Repent** therefore and be **converted,** that your sins may be blotted out . . ." (Acts 3:19). It takes both repentance and conversion for sins to be blotted out. Without true repentance there is no true conversion. This will be covered in detail in future chapters of this book.

KNOWN BY FRUIT, NOT A BUSINESS CARD

John the Baptist was the descendant of a high priest, of the tribe of Levi. When the priests and Levites of Jerusalem questioned John about who he was, he told them that he was not the Christ. "And they asked him, 'What then? Are you Elijah?' He said, 'I am not.' 'Are you the Prophet?' And he answered, 'No'" (John 1:21). John was quick to say no to the questions "Are you

Elijah?" and "Are you the Prophet?" Why did he deny
he was the Elijah prophet when the angel Gabriel and
Jesus both said he was (Luke 1:17; Matthew 17:12-13)?
One of the reasons I believe he said no was to draw the
attention of these men, who were bound to their professional ministry titles and the praise of men, back to God.

Ministry was big business then even as it is now. If
they had had the resources we have, you would have
seen them in the same rut we have been in the last part of
the twentieth century: Christian television programming
that looks and acts more like Hollywood, encouraging
Christians to be spectators, and "Christian" music that
patterns itself by the world, not by God's standards.
Many charge exorbitant amounts of money to come and
"minister." If their price cannot be met, they don't
come. They have agents who book them, not the Holy
Ghost. The emphasis is to entertain, not minister, even
though they call themselves ministers. Many defend
these musicians by saying they are getting the message
out to those who have never heard. The question is,
what is the type of message being proclaimed? A minister's life-style speaks more loudly than what he preaches
or sings! What kind of converts are being made? Those
who are forsaking all to follow Jesus, or those who have
bought a lie that they can love the world and serve Jesus
at the same time? The way we win them over is the way
we will have to maintain them.

We have Christian magazines displaying and feeding
on the competition of ministries through advertisement
of seminars and conventions. Prophet so-and-so is having his school of the prophets seminar. Come and enjoy
the attractions of the city while you attend the meetings
and become a prophet of the last days. Pastor so-and-so
is having his yearly convention. You don't want to miss

it; your life will be changed forever. They sound like they
are running a popularity contest, not a ministry. Then
when many of them do get up to preach, they spend
much time on how wonderful their ministries are and
how much good they are doing in the church. Who is
receiving the attention, the Lord or their ministries?

Paul said in Galatians 1:10, "For do I now persuade men, or God? Or do I seek to please men? **For if
I still pleased men, I would not be a bondservant of Christ.**"
The Greek word for "pleased" in this verse is *aresko.*
One of the definitions of this word from Strong's dictionary of Greek New Testament words is as follows:
"Please through the idea of exciting emotion." To put
it more plainly, that is called hype! So what is being
said here is, "If I still seek to stimulate men's emotions
through excitement (hype), I am not a bondservant of
Christ!" What is hype? It is seeking to arouse emotions through superficial stimulation. It is saying we
are in the Spirit when we are just having an emotional
high! It is saying we are in revival when revival is
nowhere to be found. It is declaring falsehood as
truth! Does this sound like today?

These men who approached John were into titles,
positions, and popularity. Controlling the people was
key to the success of their ministries. The reason they
came out to him was not to hear his message but to
check him out. They were threatened by his ministry.
The multitudes were leaving the Pharisees' religious
services to go out to the wilderness to hear this man.
That is why, when they first came to check him out, he
looked at them and called them snakes! He saw right
through their religious masks and viewed their heart
motives. He was not about to enter into their arena of
titles, positions, and motive of ministry. So when

asked by them, "Who are you, that we may give an answer to those who sent us? What do you say about yourself?" He said: "I am 'The voice of one crying in the wilderness: "Make straight the way of the LORD,"' as the prophet Isaiah said" (John 1:22-23). He immediately pointed them to the Lord and not to his ministry.

If God has put you in the ministry of a prophet, He will make it known. You will not need to advertise your position in the ministry. The Bible says about Samuel, one of the greatest prophets of the Old Testament, "And all Israel from Dan to Beersheba knew that Samuel had been established as a prophet of the Lord" (1 Samuel 3:20). Your fruit will reveal your call. So many get hung up on, "What office am I called to and what is my title?" Then once they settle on it, they begin to run their ministries as they perceive that office. Their perception could be only partially correct or totally wrong.

ALL FLESH SHALL SEE IT TOGETHER

The voice of one crying in the wilderness: "Prepare the way of the Lord; make straight in the desert a highway for our God. Every valley shall be exalted and every mountain and hill brought low; the crooked places shall be made straight and the rough places smooth; the glory of the Lord shall be revealed, and **all flesh shall see it together**; for the mouth of the Lord has spoken" (Isaiah 40:3-5).

Although this scripture was fulfilled for John the Baptist's day, he was not the total fulfillment of it. Did all flesh see the glory of the Lord in the days of John the Baptist? The answer is clearly no. Although many did see the glory of God in the person of Jesus Christ, it cannot be said that all flesh saw it together. The Bible makes it clear that the glory of the Lord will be seen by all flesh in the days of Christ's second coming.

Many of the prophecies in the Bible have more than one fulfillment. Many times there are preliminary fulfillments prior to the final fulfillment of what God says. Paul speaks of the "manifold [variegated or many-sided] wisdom of God." God's word can apply to many different situations and events. So to take a truth or prophecy from Scripture and say that it is **the** truth or **the** prophetic fulfillment will be limiting what God wants to say. This is why many in these days have trouble receiving what the prophets in the Old Testament foretold for our day. We must realize that Jesus said in Matthew 5:17, "Do not think that I came to destroy the Law or the Prophets. I did not come to destroy but to **fulfill**."

So this prophecy of Isaiah 40 again shows us that there are two different Elijah anointings. The first came prior to Jesus' first coming, and the second comes prior to His second coming.

THE VOICE OF ONE

Now you may be thinking, "Why does it say 'the voice of **one** crying . . .'"? The answer is there will be no division of purpose in these latter-days prophets and ministers. They will have one voice: the voice of

God! They will be as one man. They will be dead to
their own desires and will seek only the will of God.
They will have trained in the wilderness, and it was
there that they died to themselves and their own ministry ambitions.

God is raising up an army in these last days who are
one in purpose. The training ground for this army is the
desert, or dry places: ". . . in the desert prepare the way
for the Lord" (Isaiah 40:3, NIV). We can see the results
of the wilderness in the children of Israel after leaving
Egypt. The wilderness served two purposes for them.
First, it weeded out all those who were serving the Lord
for selfish purposes—they were scattered in the wilderness. Second, it prepared the people to go in and take the
promised land. You do not see the same rebellion and
lust in the book of Joshua as you do in the books of
Exodus and Numbers. Those who were self-seeking
were weeded out while the rest were strengthened by the
trials they faced in the desert.

My wife was awakened by the Lord a few years ago at 4
A.M. She went into our living room, and there the Lord
gave her a vision of the army He is raising up in the last
days. The men and women had the same faces (a faceless
army—no superstars). Everyone knew his position, and no
one was vying for someone else's. She told me in this vision
that everyone in the army had their heads tilted up looking
at the leader, who was Jesus. When the leader turned, the
people of the army did not have to look at one another, they
all just turned at the same time because they were following
the Master. The army was like one man because they were
one in purpose and dead to their own desires.

(Our first book, titled *Victory in the Wilderness*, would
be helpful in a more thorough understanding of this
training and preparation process.)

DO NOT BECOME CRITICAL

As you read this book, I want to encourage you not to get on the defensive but to examine your heart in sincerity. Allow the Spirit of God to reveal any areas of your life or ministry that you have compromised by tolerating sin or flesh.

I also want to say again, please do not become critical of the leaders in the body of Christ or your church. It would be foolish for you to do this, as two wrongs don't make a right. I believe the purpose for bringing these points out is to direct you, the reader, to that which God is calling you and to awaken the Church to return back to the heart of God. Becoming judgmental will not accomplish this goal.

God put young Samuel under Eli's leadership. Eli was full of compromise, and his two sons, who were also in ministry positions over Samuel, were corrupt and wicked. The corruption was so bad that the word of the Lord was rare. However, Samuel did not come out and attack the leadership personally. He did not rise up and overthrow the leadership, declaring, "He was the true prophet with the word of Lord." Instead he ". . . ministered to the Lord before Eli" (1 Samuel 3:1). God warned Eli and his sons. They did not listen, so God brought judgment. He then raised Samuel up to be leader instead of Eli.

God put David under King Saul's leadership. Saul was a domineering, insecure leader who was out to kill David. In his pursuit of David, Saul killed eighty-five priests of the Lord who wore the linen ephod because they gave David food and shelter and hid him from Saul in the city of Nob. Saul was out to destroy David and would do it at any cost! He had an army of three thousand soldiers out to accomplish his task. The day came when David and Abishai (Joab's little brother) secretly came into Saul's camp while they were asleep. David came to Saul, who was sleeping, and Abishai said to David, "God has delivered your enemy into your hand this day. Now therefore please, let me strike him at once with the spear." But David replied by saying, "Do not destroy him; **for who can stretch out his hand against the Lord's anointed, and be guiltless?**" David would not judge the Lord's servant. He let God do it! God did judge Saul, and he was slain by the Philistines at Mount Gilboa. When David heard it, he did not rejoice but rather mourned and sang a song for Saul and had the entire army join with him in it.

God is the One who will judge His servants. Do not become critical of His servants and speak out against them. You must minister to the Lord. If you have areas in your life that He is dealing with, let them be dealt with. He will take care of His servants.

4 PREPARE THE WAY OF THE LORD

We have attracted sinners with a message powerless to liberate them.

> The voice of one crying in the wilderness: "**Prepare** the way of the LORD; make straight in the desert a highway for our God. Every valley shall be exalted and every mountain and hill brought low; the **crooked** places shall be made straight and the rough places smooth; the glory of the Lord shall be revealed, and all flesh shall see it together; for the mouth of the Lord has spoken." Isaiah 40:3-5

As already stated, these scriptures prophetically speak of the ministry of John the Baptist. "For this is he who was spoken of by the prophet Isaiah, saying: '**The voice of one crying in the wilderness:** Prepare the way of the Lord; make His paths straight'" (Matthew 3:3).

The Hebrew word for prepare in Isaiah 40:4 is *panah*. The definition of this word from the Hebrew dictionary is "to turn, return, or prepare." In forty-nine other places in the Old Testament this word is translated "turn" or "return." In only six places in the Old Testament is this word translated "prepare." (Four of these have to do with this same message of the way of the Lord—Isaiah 40:3, 57:14, 62:10; Malachi 3:1.) The words "prepare" and "prepared" are found more than one hundred times in the Old Testament but from different Hebrew words. Therefore, it is safe to say that this verse could have read, "The voice of one crying in the wilderness: 'Return to the way of the LORD. . . .'"

In Isaiah 40:4 it is said that "the **crooked** places shall be made straight . . . ." The Hebrew word for "crooked" is *aqob*. The definition of this word from the Hebrew dictionary is "fraudulent, deceitful, polluted, or crooked." *Aqob* appears three times in the Old Testament. The first is the above mentioned scripture; the second is Jeremiah 17:9, which reads, "The heart is **deceitful [aqob]** above all things, and desperately wicked; who can know it?" The third is Hosea 6:8, where it is translated "polluted." I believe another way of reading Isaiah 40:4 could be as follows: "The **deceitful** places shall be made straight . . . ."

Putting this together, it would read as follows, "The voice of one crying in the wilderness, return to the way of the Lord . . . The deceitful places shall be made straight . . ." (Isaiah 40:3-4).

When we return to the ministry of John the Baptist, we find that the angel Gabriel said of John, "And he will **turn** many of the children of Israel to the Lord their God" (Luke 1:16). He was not sent to the gentiles who had never known the name of the Lord. He was sent to the lost sheep in the religious structure and those who had left the religious structure because of discontent, discouragement, or offense. The thrust of his ministry was to call the children of Israel to **return** to the ways of God and not to continue in their own ways, even though many were religious and believed with all their hearts that they were fine in their present state. Thousands attended synagogue faithfully, totally unaware of the true condition of their hearts. They were **deceived**, thinking their worship and service to the Lord was acceptable to God. John was sent to expose this deception in which they trusted. They believed they were justified because they were Abraham's descendants who adhered to the doctrines of the elders, paying tithes, praying prayers, and performing countless other religious habits, yet these were only a substitute, when in reality their hearts were far from God. They were **deceived**.

Once again, as with the people of John's day, many today are deceived. They are not pursuing God but their own gain. However, often they do this in the name of the Lord with scriptures to back up their case. Jesus has been incorporated into their life-style for self-improvement. They believe regardless of the life-style they now lead that because they have prayed a sinner's prayer, attend a church, pay tithes, and speak in tongues, they stand justified and ready for His return. They are **deceived**.

These people are the offspring of the gospel of self. Our message has been, "Come to Jesus and get . . . ." We have attracted sinners with a message powerless to liberate them from sin. We've solicited them by promising a new and improved life-style. We have been more concerned with a positive response from the people than watching the truth set them free. We draw sinners by enticing them with the perks or benefits of salvation without clearly showing them where they are and then bringing a message of repentance so they'll turn to the Lordship of Jesus Christ.

Jeremiah 9:3-6 says, "**They are not valiant for the truth on the earth.** For they proceed from evil to evil, and they do not know Me,' says the LORD . . . 'Everyone will **deceive his neighbor**, and will not speak the truth; they have **taught their tongue to speak lies**; they weary themselves to commit iniquity. Your dwelling place is in the **midst of deceit; through deceit they refuse to know Me**,' says the Lord."

Where are the men and women who are **valiant for truth** on the earth? This question is a cry of the heart of God. Instead of standing up for righteousness, ministers and other Christians are concerned that they may offend people by proclaiming truth; instead they back off and teach their tongues to speak lies. What is alarming is the fact that if a person continues in a lie he will eventually begin to believe it as truth. This is deception! James 1:26 confirms this by saying: "If anyone among you thinks he is religious, and does not bridle his tongue but **deceives his own heart**, this one's religion is useless." This leaven of compromise has spread to such a great extent that even ministers are persecuted by other ministers for speaking truth. It is easier to gain converts if you don't say anything possibly offensive to them—which often means you cannot tell the truth. Ministers settle for messages that attract people to Jesus without repentance. As a result, sin is still very much alive in the **hearts** of the people.

This results in "Christians" who believe the lie that you can serve God and love the world too! This gives them a form of godliness while denying its power to change hearts. Study the following verse carefully:

> But know this, that in the last days per-
> ilous times will come: For men will be
> lovers of themselves, lovers of money,
> boasters, proud, blasphemers, disobedi-
> ent to parents, unthankful, unholy, unlov-

ing, unforgiving, slanderers, without self-
control, brutal, despisers of good, traitors,
headstrong, haughty, lovers of pleasure
rather than lovers of God, **having a form of
godliness but denying its power** . . . always
learning and never able to come to the
knowledge of the truth (2 Timothy 3:1-7).

I have heard ministers use this scripture to say
men and women would have a form of godliness but
reject the gifts of the Spirit. But upon closer inspec-
tion we find this is not what is being said. God is saying in the last days (in which we are currently living)
people in the Church will call on the name of the
Lord, attend church, even be excited about the
promises of God yet deny the power of godliness **to
change them from being**: lovers of themselves to lovers
of others; lovers of money to lovers of God; proud
and boastful to truly humble; disobedient to parents
to obedient; unthankful to thankful; unholy to holy;
unloving to loving, etc. Paul describes them as
"always learning and never able to come to the
knowledge of the truth." In other words, they love
learning about the things of God but will never come
to the knowledge of the truth because they do not
apply it. Thus they remain unchanged. Though they
appear to have a spiritual life, they actually do not
know God because of deceit! God says, ". . . **through
deceit they refuse to know Me**" (Jeremiah 9:6). This
form of godliness does not bring intimate knowledge
of Him. Jesus said many would say to Him in that
day, "'Lord, Lord, have we not prophesied in Your
name, cast out demons in Your name, and done
many wonders in Your name?' And then I will declare

to them, '**I never knew you; depart from Me, you who practice lawlessness!**'" (Matthew 7:22-23).

First Corinthians 6:9-10 says: "Do you not know that the unrighteous will not inherit the kingdom of God? **Do not be deceived.** Neither fornicators, nor idolaters, nor adulterers, nor homosexuals, nor sodomites, nor thieves, nor covetous, nor drunkards, nor revilers, nor extortioners will inherit the kingdom of God."

An important point to be made: God looks at the heart. The true state of a person is determined by his heart not his actions. Jesus is returning for a holy Church, not a lukewarm, sin-filled Church! One of the definitions of holiness is "the state of being pure." Jesus said, "Blessed are the **pure in heart**, for they shall see God" (Matthew 5:8). Notice He did not say, "Blessed are the **pure in actions**, for they shall see God." We have tried to attain holiness through rules and regulations, restricting ourselves with legalistic rulings over tangible things (i.e., no make-up, strict dress code, no television sets, etc.) to obtain inward purity. But God is not looking for an outward form of holiness; He wants an inward change of your heart, for a pure heart will produce pure conduct! Jesus said in Matthew 23:26, ". . . first cleanse the inside of the cup and dish [the heart], that the outside of them may be clean also."

If your heart is pure, you will not desire to dress in a way that is seductive. A woman can wear a dress that reaches her ankles and still have a seducing spirit about her, while another woman can wear a pair of pants and have a pure heart! No matter what fashion may say, it is not the clothes that make the woman, but the woman who makes the clothes.

A man can boast that he has never been divorced, yet lust after other women. Is this holiness?

If your heart is pure you will not desire or tolerate sin. Yet you will not condemn with a self-righteous attitude those who are bound by sin! Often we categorize sin, condemning specific sins while excusing others. Setting ourselves up as judges, we become like the Pharisee who condemned the tax collector and others while justifying himself.

Galations 5:19-21 says: "Now the works of the flesh are evident, which are: adultery, fornication, uncleanness, lewdness, idolatry, sorcery, **hatred, contentions, jealousies, outbursts of wrath, selfish ambitions,** dissensions, heresies, envy, murders, drunkenness, revelries, and the like; of which I tell you beforehand, just as I also told you in time past, that **those who practice such things will not inherit the kingdom of God.**"

Hatred, strife, jealousy, outbursts of wrath, and selfish ambitions are included in the same list as adultery and murder. Many times self-righteous people will condemn a homosexual while they themselves are eaten up with bitterness and hatred. This hatred is seen in their attitude toward the homosexual whom Jesus died for. The person eaten with hatred is no more righteous than a person bound by homosexuality! (This is discussed in detail in the upcoming chapters.)

The Elijah anointing that God is bringing in these last days will boldly confront these deceptions. The message will be to *return* to the way of the Lord, and as a result, "the deceitful places shall be made straight . . ." (Isaiah 40:3-4). God loves His Church too much to leave it in deception.

EVERY MOUNTAIN AND HILL BROUGHT LOW

The voice of one crying in the wilderness: "Prepare the way of the LORD;

make straight in the desert a highway for
our God. Every valley shall be exalted and
every mountain and hill brought low; the
crooked places shall be made straight and
the rough places smooth" (Isaiah 40:4).

God says every valley shall be exalted and every
mountain and hill brought low! Mountains and hills
speak of the pride of men. Every proud and lofty way
will be made low.

We must define what pride is. Boldness is often
mistaken for pride. If a man is confident in God, often
it is taken as arrogance and pride. When David came
to the battlefield where his brothers were fighting and
saw the giant defying the armies of God, his response
of confidence caused his older brothers to accuse him
of pride. David said, "What shall be done for the man
who kills this Philistine and takes away the reproach
from Israel? For who is this uncircumcised Philistine,
that he should defy the armies of the living God?" (1
Samuel 17:26).

His boldness brought conviction to his eldest brother
Eliab, who had been faithfully serving in King Saul's
army. "Eliab's **anger** was aroused against David, and he
said, 'Why did you come down here? And with whom
have you left those few sheep in the wilderness? **I know
your pride** and the insolence of your heart . . .'" (1
Samuel 17:28). Eliab was the one who was proud.
Perhaps he was still a little upset because Samuel had
anointed his kid brother as the next king of Israel instead
of him. Was this the reason God had not chosen Eliab—
a proud heart? Many times we accuse others of the
things we fight in ourselves.

So it is today. Many who are confident in God are

accused of being proud. There is a false concept of pride and humility. Many in the Church think humility is to act cautiously, to conduct yourself super-spiritually, acting as if you are unworthy. They have brought humility to an outward act when it should be an inward state of your heart.

There was a king of Judah named Uzziah, a descendant of King David. Uzziah was crowned king at sixteen years of age. When he became king, he sought God diligently. Of course, if you were sixteen and were made king of a nation, you would seek God too. It is recorded of him that ". . . as long as he sought the Lord, **God made him prosper**" (2 Chronicles 26:5). God greatly blessed him; he made war against the Philistines and defeated them in numerous cities, as well as the Arabians, Meunites, and Ammonites. He led the nation to become very strong economically as well as militarily. Much success was experienced under his leadership.

> But when **he was strong** his **heart was lifted up,** to his destruction, for he transgressed against the Lord his God **by entering the temple of the Lord to burn incense on the altar of incense** (2 Chronicles 26:16).

It was when Uzziah was strong, not weak, that his heart was lifted up in pride. It was when he saw prosperity and success come upon everything he undertook that his heart ceased seeking the Lord! God spoke to me one day and said, "John, most who have fallen have fallen in the abundant times not the dry times." This is a trap that many Christians fall into. When they first get saved, they hunger to know the Lord and His ways. They seek and trust Him for everything. They come to church, crying, "Lord, I want to know You!" However, when they come to the place where they have amassed knowledge and become strong in their experiences, their attitude changes to "let's see if this minister has got it!" Now, instead of reading their Bibles with the attitude, "Lord, reveal Yourself to me," they have their doctrine established and read what they believe instead of believing what they read. They are now experts in the Scriptures but have forfeited the humility of heart they once had.

This is the case in America with so much teaching available to us. Corinthians 8:1 says, "We know that we all have knowledge. **Knowledge puffs up [pride]**, but love edifies." Love seeks not its own! Pride seeks its own, often masked in religion! God says knowledge gained without love results in pride.

As King Uzziah became more proud, he became more religious! His heart was lifted up and he entered the temple to "worship." Pride and a religious spirit go hand in hand. A religious spirit causes a person to think he is humble through his appearance of "spirituality," when the truth is he is proud. On the other hand, pride keeps a person in bondage to a religious spirit because he is too proud to admit it! This is one reason why pride in the Church is so well camouflaged. It hides behind a religious mask.

Religious pride could be defined as "viewing yourself with the ability to be like God, apart from God." It is seeing oneself as having the ability to do, know, or have anything your way (even if it seems spiritual), apart from God's way. This causes you to be the source and center of everything in your life. To further explain this, look at how Jesus viewed Himself.

> Then Jesus answered and said to them,
> "Most assuredly, I say to you, **the Son can
> do nothing of Himself,** but what He **sees the
> Father do**; for whatever He does, the Son
> also does in like manner" (John 5:19).

That says it all. Even Jesus said He could do nothing apart from His Father's direction, empowerment, and help. Notice the tense of what He said. He did not say, "The Son can do nothing of Himself, but what He **saw** the Father do." Rather, He said, "The Son can do nothing of Himself, but what He **sees** the Father **do**." A religious spirit will hold fast to what God did while resisting what God is doing. Working hand in hand with this religious spirit is pride, which operates in the power of its own strength.

We see an example of this in the Pharisees. They acted very holy, while their hearts were filled with pride. They held on to what God had done through Moses and Abraham, while resisting the Son of the living God manifested among them. Their appearance was very spiritual . . . fasting weekly, tithing, praying long prayers in public. However, these were done in their own ability, all in the name of Jehovah with Old Testament scriptures to support them, but not in the Spirit of Jehovah!

Today, we also have those who speak in tongues, tithe, and attend church. For many years they have attended and served in the church, yet their hearts are filled with pride. They say what they do is inspired by God, but in reality it is their will and way, all in the name of Jesus!

Let's look again at Uzziah and see what happened when he was confronted by the priests.

> **Then Uzziah became furious;** and he had a
> censer in his hand to burn incense. And

while he was **angry with the priests, leprosy broke out** on his forehead, before the priests in the house of the Lord, beside the incense altar. And Azariah the chief priest and all the priests looked at him, and there, on his forehead, he was leprous; so they thrust him out of that place. Indeed he also hurried to get out, because the Lord had struck him (2 Chronicles 26:19).

Uzziah became furious. Pride always justifies itself. This self-defense will be coupled with anger. A proud person will blame everyone else while he excuses himself. Uzziah's anger was directed at the priests, but the problem did not lie in them but with him. Pride had blinded his eyes! As a result, leprosy broke out on his body. Leprosy was an outward manifestation of an inward condition! So leprosy is what appeared, but the root of it was *pride*. The same is true today. We have seen many ministers falling into sin, especially sexual sins. The Lord spoke to me about all the sexual sins among ministers: He said, "John, the root is not sexual, the root is pride; the sexual sin is a result of the seed of pride already grounded in their hearts."

God is raising the prophetic anointing as "the voice of one crying in the wilderness; return to the way of the Lord . . . Every valley shall be exalted and **every** mountain and hill brought low." Pride will be leveled before the glory of the Lord is revealed. Isaiah 6:1 says: "**In the year that King Uzziah died, I saw the Lord** sitting on a throne, high and lifted up, and the train of His robe filled the temple." The train of His robe is a type of His glory! God spoke to me and said, "John, Isaiah did not see the glory of the Lord until Uzziah died." This message translates to us today as, "**The Church will not see God's glory until pride dies!**"

EVERY VALLEY SHALL BE EXALTED

The voice of one crying in the wilderness: "Prepare the way of the Lord; make straight in the desert a highway for our God. **Every valley shall be exalted** and every mountain and hill brought low; the crooked places shall be made straight and the rough places smooth" (Isaiah 40:3-4).

Valleys speak of humility. Those who have humbled themselves will be exalted. This is a good opportunity to say that **the wilderness will help us humble ourselves!** If you remember, it wasn't until the prodigal son had lost all his money and was eating pig's food that he came to his senses and realized everything he had pursued in this world was empty and lifeless, and true joy could be found only at his father's house.

Moses tried to deliver Israel from Egypt *his* way when he was forty years old. He knew he was the one God had called to do it! Even though he was God's choice, he attempted to do it in the strength and wisdom of Egypt. That mountain of self-ability had to be brought low. However, after forty years on the backside of the wilderness tending sheep, he was ready to do it God's way! The wilderness helped him to humble himself under God's mighty hand.

The prophet Jonah went the route of ease, running from that to which God had called him. However, after three days in the belly of a great fish, he came to his senses, humbled himself, and cried out, "Yet I will look again toward Your holy temple" (Jonah 2:4). Jonah is the one who humbled himself, but the circumstances sure helped him do it. Being in that whale's gut was definitely a wilderness experience, and it prepared the way of the Lord, not the way of Jonah! Once Jonah humbled himself, God exalted him to bring the word of the Lord to the wicked city of Nineveh.

How can we the Church point our finger at the world and preach, "Repent . . ." in the state we are in? Pride and selfish motives run rampant in ministries. We are torn by strife and division, separating us into hundreds of camps. Proverbs 13:10 says: **"By pride comes nothing but strife . . . ."** The root of the strife and division in the Church today is pride! This pride has been hidden by a false humility, saying, "We give God the glory for what He has done." But what is not spoken but still made clear is "look real good at whom He has done it through!"

As we choose to humble ourselves, just as with Jonah, God will anoint us as a people and Church to proclaim His word to this world. Then we will see the great harvest of souls. God is preparing His Church to manifest His glory as never before. Whole cities and towns will come to the Lord. Nations will come to the feet of the Master with great joy. Every one in the true Church will be involved in this great harvest. However, no flesh will glory in His sight! Men will not be able to market this great move of God nor take credit for it. Flesh will not share the glory with God!

God brought the prophet Ezekiel to the valley of dry bones and asked him what he saw. Ezekiel saw very dry bones: all the flesh had been removed! This represented the whole house of Israel. God removed every bit of the pride of flesh in the valley of humility! The people said,

"Our bones are dry, our hope is lost, and we ourselves are cut off!" They looked so hopeless that when God, who can do all things, looked at Ezekiel and said, "Can these bones live?" Ezekiel probably thought to himself, "They look so hopeless they will never live, but I don't dare say that to God about His people." So he was wise and answered, "O Lord God, only You know." Then God said, "Prophesy to these bones, and say to them, O dry bones, hear the word of the Lord!" Now if Ezekiel would have prophesied to these bones according to today's standard, we would see him go to each bone saying something like this: "Little bone, please stand up. 'Thus saith the Lord, my little bone, you are called of me and will have a ministry and marry another little bone over there that is blonde and has blue eyes, and I will give you a nice two-story house, and you will be so blessed.'" Then he would have gone to the next little bone, giving it a wonderful word of "exhortation" and so on. We have so misinterpreted the prophet's office! Ezekiel preached the word of the Lord under divine inspiration, and the prophetic word of the Lord caused breath to enter back into them and live.

So I prophesied as He commanded me, and breath came into them, and they lived, and stood upon their feet, **an exceedingly great army** (Ezekiel 37:10).

God has allowed the true Church, not the harlot Church, to come to the place that she almost seems powerless (compared to the book of Acts). He has done it to bring us to humility so that when we are filled with His power and glory, we won't fall into the same condemnation of the devil (1 Timothy 3:6), which was pride.

Joseph as a young man was a bit proud even though he loved God. When God gave him the two dreams of him ruling over his brothers, he immediately went to them and boasted of his call. However, after thirteen years of slavery and Pharaoh's dungeon, he was brought to a place where he humbled himself. When his brothers returned to him, he didn't say, "See, I told you God called me to be a leader over you." Instead he graciously gave to them and served them, as a leader in God's kingdom is called to do!

There are many in the Church who will be forerunners as Joseph was. They will go through a severe wilderness while others in the Church will not experience what these men in training have to endure. Then, when these leaders are ready, God will bring the rest into a wilderness of a draught. They will no longer be able to live as they once had. They will come to these forerunners, as Joseph's brothers did, and leadership will change hands! Leaders who formerly ruled by domination will now come to those they once dominated and serve under their leadership! However, the character of God will have been developed in their lives due to their valley of humility, and they will not seek to be served, but rather to serve! God will now be able to exalt them, for He can trust them to be humble in heart, turning to the children and not to themselves. God says this Elijah prophetic anointing will "'. . . turn the hearts of the fathers [leaders] to the children,' and the disobedient to the wisdom of the just . . ." (Luke 1:17).

Listen carefully, all who call on the name of the Lord. You will either humble yourself in the valley of humility, or you will be brought low on the day His glory is revealed! Every valley will be exalted, and every mountain and hill will be brought low!

5 WOLVES IN SHEEP'S CLOTHING

Balaam's fruit was evil even though his prophecies were correct.

"Beware of **false prophets**, who come to you in **sheep's clothing**, but inwardly they are ravenous **wolves. You will know them by their fruits.** Do men gather grapes from thornbushes or figs from thistles? Even so, every good tree bears good fruit, but a bad tree bears bad fruit. A good tree cannot bear bad fruit, nor can a bad tree bear good fruit. Every tree that does not bear good fruit is cut down and thrown into the fire. **Therefore by their fruits you will know them.**"   Matthew 7:15-20

IDENTIFYING FALSE PROPHETS

Jesus warned us by saying "beware" of false prophets! Why are we warned so often in the New Testament? The reason is they are deceptive. They are subtle and crafty, not blatant. They come in sheep's clothing, not wolves'

clothing. They look, talk, and act like Christians. Jesus said
concerning the last days that ". . . **many** false prophets will
rise up and **deceive many**" (Matthew 24:11). He went on to
say that, if possible, even the elect would be deceived by
them because of their signs and wonders. How can we
know them? Jesus said we would know them by their
fruits, not by their teachings or signs and wonders.

Let me make this important point: Jesus did not say
we would know false prophets because their prophecies
were false, or that we would know true prophets by the
fact that their prophecies did come true. This thinking
comes from Old Testament scriptures such as
Deuteronomy 18:22, which says, "When a prophet
speaks in the name of the Lord, if the thing does not
happen or come to pass, that is the thing which the Lord
has not spoken; the prophet has spoken it presumptu-
ously; you shall not be afraid of him." Many today judge
true and false prophets by this reference rather than the
reference Jesus gave us. I have heard numerous people,
even leaders, say that a man was a false prophet because
he gave a prophecy that did not come to pass. And on
the contrary, I have heard people, say, "I know this man
is a true prophet because what he said came to pass."

However, let me point out that in the Old Testament,
Baalam—who was a corrupt prophet with a covetous
heart—prophesied accurately over Israel and the birth of the
Messiah. Even though his prophetic words were accurate,
his fruit was evil. For Jesus said of him that he ". . . taught
Balak to put a stumbling block before the children of Israel,
to eat things sacrificed to idols, and to commit sexual
immorality (Revelation 2:14). He was paid money and gifts
to curse Israel, but because he could not curse whom God
had blessed, he taught Balak how to bring the children of
Israel under a curse by enticing them to sin. This would

cause them to come under judgment. As a result, twenty-four thousand children of Israel died from the plague that came as judgment on their disobedience (Numbers 23:8). Balaam's fruit was evil even though his prophecies were correct. He was a false prophet, and in Joshua 13:22 he was called a "soothsayer" and was killed by the edge of Israel's sword in battle. So as we can see, to use the accuracy of a man's prophecies to determine if he is a true or false prophet doesn't work, even in the Old Testament. Let's closely examine God's criteria in the Old Testament for discerning between true and false prophets.

> "If there arises among you a prophet or a dreamer of dreams, and he gives you a sign or a wonder, and **the sign or the wonder comes to pass,** of which he spoke to you, saying, 'Let us go after other gods'—which you have not known—'and let us serve them,' you shall not listen to the words of that prophet or that dreamer of dreams, for the Lord your God is testing you to know whether you love the Lord your God with all your heart and with all your soul. You shall walk after the Lord your God and fear Him, and keep His commandments and obey His voice, and you shall serve Him and hold fast to Him. But that prophet or that dreamer of dreams shall be put to death, because he has spoken in order to **turn you away from the Lord your God,** who brought you out of the land of Egypt and redeemed you from the house of bondage, to **entice** you from the way in which the Lord your God commanded you to walk.

So you shall put away the evil from your
midst" (Deuteronomy 13:1-5).

The fruit of Balaam's life and ministry turned the
children of Israel away from the heart of the Lord, even
though what he prophesied was true and accurate. So it
should now be made plain that even though a person's
words are accurate, it is not a confirmation that he or she
is a true prophet. Jesus made it clear by saying,
"Therefore by their fruits you will know them"
(Matthew 7:20). What must be examined is the fruit of
the minister's life as well as the fruit of his ministry.

YOU WILL KNOW THEM BY THEIR FRUITS

Galatians 5:22-23 says, "But the fruit of the Spirit is
love, joy, peace, longsuffering, kindness, goodness, faithfulness, gentleness, self-control. Against such there is no
law." This is the fruit that must be seen in the personal
life of a true prophet. Jesus said that the world would
know that we are His disciples by our love one for another
(John 13:35). To love someone doesn't necessarily mean
to be nice to them. There are con artists who make a person feel wonderful and treat them nice in order to take
advantage of them. There are men who will treat women
wonderfully, but only to gain a sexual advantage over
them. So just because a person smiles and says nice
things about you doesn't mean he or she is walking in the
fruit of the Spirit! Second Corinthians 5:16 says,
"Henceforth know we no man after the flesh . . . ." We are
not to know men and women by their personalities.
Personalities can be deceptive. Rather, we are to know
them by the Spirit. The fruit of the Spirit must be dis-

cerned. To discern is to see or recognize clearly the
motives and intentions of a person. To discern is to accurately perceive what is in another's heart. The Bible says
that those who are spiritually mature have their senses
exercised to discern both good and evil (Hebrews 5:14).
In order to properly discern, your motive must be love,
not criticalness. Many people claim that they can discern
evil in others, but in reality they are only critical.
Philippians 1:9 says, "And this I pray, that your **love** may
abound still more and more in knowledge and **all discernment.**" We see here proper discernment is rooted in the
love of God.

When Jesus says "you will know false prophets by
their fruits," He is saying you can discern them by the
fruit of their lives. Is it love or selfishness masked by a
smile? True love is not self-seeking. It is not motivated
by personal gain or pleasure. It is not motivated by success, recognition, status, or money. It will speak and perform the truth even if it means being rejected, because it
seeks the best for the other. If you truly love someone,
you are willing to lay down your desires and goals for the
best interest of the other. Jesus said in John 15:13,
"Greater love has no one than this, than to lay down
one's life for his friends." This is the fruit that Jesus says
we must see in the true prophet's life.

We must also look at the fruit produced by the ministry. Is it drawing people closer to God? Or is it pointing
the people to the ministry by speaking words the people
want to hear rather than what they need to hear? Jeremiah
cries out by the Spirit of God, saying, "Also I have seen a
horrible thing in the prophets of Jerusalem: They commit
adultery and walk in lies; **they also strengthen the hands of
evildoers, so that no one turns back from his wickedness**"
(Jeremiah 23:14). How were they strengthening the

hands of the evildoers? By preaching to them what would please them rather than confronting their wickedness. This runs rampant today in America. Pastors and ministers preach nonconvicting sermons so that people will not become offended and leave. If they leave, they will take their money with them. The deception: "We need their tithes, offerings, or talents to continue this ministry God has entrusted to us." Because they compromise the truth, they begin to believe the deception of lukewarmness. The result or fruit of this: No one turns back or repents from the wicked thoughts they have in their hearts or their wicked conduct which is so evident. Then if someone comes along and preaches the truth, these ministers and church members begin to shun it by saying, "Their preaching is too hard. They are not being loving." God is very merciful; that is why He allows us to repent!

There was a couple who gave sizable gifts into our ministry during our first couple of years on the road. They loved our ministry and told many about us. They always looked forward to my coming to their area to minister. A day came when the Lord gave me a message of correction for them. They were attempting to control the church with their influence and money. The lady did not like what I said at all. She became offended over it and quit supporting our ministry. So did her family. I knew they were no longer supporting us as a result of what I did, but telling them the truth was more important for them, and the church, even though they did not see it that way. After two months of considering this situation, I felt impressed to write a letter. I strengthened the message I had given her and added some words that God had put on my heart. I didn't care about their money or rejection; what mattered was the truth. When God is your source, people cannot manipulate you with their money or friendship. Look at what God said through the prophet Micah.

> This is what the Lord says: "As for the prophets (ministers) who **lead my people astray, if one feeds them, they proclaim 'peace'; if he does not, they prepare to wage war against him.** Therefore night will come over you, without visions, and darkness, without divination. The sun will set for the prophets (ministers), and the day will go dark for them. The seers will be ashamed and the diviners disgraced. They will all cover their faces because **there is no answer from God.**" But as for me, **I am filled with power, with the Spirit of the Lord, and with justice and might, to declare to Jacob his transgression, to Israel his sin.** Hear this, you leaders of the house of Jacob, you rulers of the house of Israel, who despise justice and distort all that is right; who build Zion with bloodshed, and Jerusalem with wickedness. **Her leaders judge for a bribe, her priests teach for a price, and her prophets tell fortunes for money. Yet they lean upon the Lord and say, "Is not the Lord among us? No disaster will come upon us"** (Micah 3:5-11).

This sounds like what has been happening in the Church of America. If a person is a sizable donor to a ministry, the minister and ministry team will tolerate behavior out of him that they would never tolerate out of a person who was poor or who did not have fame or influence. They will put men like this on their board or give them a reserved seat or preferential treatment.

James addresses this by saying, "My brethren, do not hold the faith of our Lord Jesus Christ, the Lord of glory, with partiality. For if there should come into your assembly a man with gold rings, in fine apparel, and there should also come in a poor man in filthy clothes, and you **pay attention** to the one wearing the fine clothes and say to him, 'You sit here in a good place,' and say to the poor man, 'You stand there,' or, 'Sit here at my footstool,' have you not shown partiality among yourselves, and become judges with evil thoughts?" (James 2:1-4).

Sad to say, money talks in many of the churches and ministries of America. Special attention is given to those who have it. Banquets and functions are given for the "high donors" to ministries. For what purpose? So they will keep giving and not be drawn into another ministry, thereby taking their support elsewhere! Now the minister is no longer controlled by the Spirit of God but by his wealthy donors. He will speak well to the ones who feed his ministry, while overlooking their sins. Now these wealthy people have influence in the ministry. This is not to say that *all* ministers who give appreciation banquets and special functions do so to raise money—some genuinely want to reach out to those who have invested in their work. However, if a banquet is given, it should be for those who give one dollar a month to the ministry as well as those who give five hundred dollars a month. Jesus said the widow woman gave more than all the rest even though she only gave two mites! If banquets are done with this motive they would have a totally different atmosphere about them.

God makes it clear how dangerous it is to receive the bribes of the rich or influential people: "And you shall take no bribe, for a bribe **blinds the discerning** and **perverts the**

words of the righteous" (Exodus 23:8). A minister loses his ability to discern the moment he begins to give preferential treatment to the one who has influence or money. His discernment is gone because he is motivated by selfishness, not love. His words become perverted and thus the ministry begins to backslide from that moment on, even though the ministry may continue to GROW and the anointing doesn't wane. Oh, yes, the anointing does not stop because ". . . the gifts and the calling of God are irrevocable" (Romans 11:29). God doesn't take the anointing and call away. That is why we have some ministers, still walking in the power and anointing of God, whose lives are perverted.

Micah was one who truly loved the people. He said that because the ministers were speaking peace to the ones who fed them, they would have no answer from the Lord. Their words sounded as if they were from God, but in reality they were not. However, because Micah was courageous enough to speak what God was saying—knowing he would be persecuted for it— he was filled with power and the Spirit of the Lord. He had the answer from the Lord that the others tried to imitate. He was therefore able to rebuke them, correct them, or exhort them. He was able to minister what God was saying rather than what would serve his ministry's best interest. In his case the word of the Lord was to expose the sins of God's people and call them to repentance. He did not minister smooth words in order to receive acceptance but preached what God was saying whether the people liked it or not.

God is raising up a generation that will speak what He is saying, even if it is an unpopular message. These ministers will be young and old alike. Some will have been in the ministry several years; others will be newcomers. They will have the fruit of the Spirit in their personal lives. They will have had the character of God developed in their lives. The love of God will be the foundation of their lives and ministries. Therefore, they will love His people with a pure love. Their pursuit will not be the gifts or the ministry but the heart of God. For they know that "though I speak with the tongues of men and of angels, but have not love, I have become sounding brass or a clanging cymbal. And though I have the gift of prophecy, and understand all mysteries and all knowledge, and though I have all faith, so that I could remove mountains, but have not love, I am nothing. And though I bestow all my goods to feed the poor, and though I give my body to be burned, but have not love, it profits me nothing" (1 Corinthians 13:1-3). Knowing this, they will "**pursue** love, and **desire** spiritual gifts . . ." (1 Corinthians 14:1).

The New Testament speaks of "false apostles" and "false brethren" (2 Corinthians 11:13, 26). Both were judged by the fruit of their personal lives and the fruit produced by their ministries. Were their ministries drawing people to themselves or to the plan and purpose of God? However, Paul, a true apostle, exhorted Timothy: "But you have carefully followed my doctrine, manner of life, purpose, faith, longsuffering, love, perseverance" (2 Timothy 3:10). Even though there were tremendous miracles and gifts in Paul's ministry, he reminded Timothy that he had followed the fruit of the Spirit in Paul's life, not the miracles or anointing. Jesus made it absolutely clear by saying: "By this all will know that you are My disciples, if you have love for one another" (John 13:35).

So again I will say, don't look at the miracles or anointing to determine if you are dealing with a false or true prophet, apostle, or brother, but look at the fruit of his personal life and ministry.

6 DEPART FROM ME: I NEVER KNEW YOU

Who are these *many* not granted entrance to the kingdom?

"**Beware of false prophets,** who come to you in sheep's clothing, but inwardly they are ravenous wolves. You will know them by their fruits. Do men gather grapes from thornbushes or figs from thistles? Even so, every good tree bears good fruit, but a bad tree bears bad fruit. A good tree cannot bear bad fruit, nor [can] a bad tree bear good fruit. Every tree that does not bear good fruit is cut down and thrown into the fire. Therefore by their fruits you will know them.

"**Not everyone who says to Me, 'Lord, Lord,' shall enter the kingdom of heaven,** but he who does the **will of My Father** in heaven. **Many** will say to Me in that day, 'Lord, Lord, have we not prophesied in **Your name**, cast out demons in **Your name**, and done many wonders in **Your name**?' And then I will declare to them, 'I never knew

you; depart from Me, you who **practice**
lawlessness!'"

Matthew 7:15-23

"MANY WILL SAY TO ME IN THAT DAY"

Jesus made it clear we would know false prophets by
their fruit. As discussed in the last chapter, we can discern them by the fruit in their personal lives and the
fruit of their ministries. We see here that the fruit of
ministry that Jesus was looking for was not signs, wonders, or miracles; if it was He would have welcomed
them because they prophesied, cast out devils, and
performed miracles in the name of Jesus. The fruit
produced by the ministry of a true prophet or any of
the other fivefold ministry gifts we are to look for is
obedience to the will of God. That is why He says,
"Not everyone who says to Me, 'Lord, Lord,' shall
enter the kingdom of heaven, **but he who does the will of
My Father in heaven.**"

These false prophets will lead many astray by deception. They themselves will be deceived because they will
not be doers of the will or Word of God. James 1:22 says,
"But be doers of the word, and not hearers only, **deceiving yourselves.**" They themselves will be deceived, thinking that what they do will grant them an entrance to the
kingdom of God. Paul tells Timothy, "But evil men and
impostors will grow worse and worse, **deceiving and being
deceived**" (2 Timothy 3:13). The dictionary defines
"impostor" as one who deceives others by an assumed
character or false pretenses. The character they assume
is a true minister of Jesus Christ, but in reality they are
wolves in sheep's clothing. They themselves are deceived

and in their deception deceive others. They are the blind leading the blind into the pit.

Jesus said that many would come to Him in that day calling Him "Lord" but would not be granted entrance into the kingdom. These many will be deceived by the false prophets. Jesus warned us about this in Matthew 24:11-12:

> "Then **many false prophets** [wolves in sheep's clothing] will rise up and **deceive many** [the many who will say in that day, 'Lord, Lord,']. And because lawlessness will abound, the **love** of many will grow cold."

The question is, who are these many not granted entrance to the kingdom? Are these Buddhists, Muslims, witches and warlocks, or men and women of other cults? The answer is plainly **no** for the following reasons.

They will look at the Lord Jesus and say they did miracles and cast out devils in His name. Not in the name of Mohammed or Buddha, nor by the power of Satan. In Matthew 12:26 Jesus explained, "If Satan casts out Satan, he is divided against himself. How then will his kingdom stand?" Jesus clarified that Satan will not cast out Satan. The many who come to Jesus on the day of judgment will have cast out devils in Jesus' name!

Could these be men and women who use the name of Jesus just to work miracles and cast out demons without any other association with the Lord Jesus? To answer this question let's look at an instance in the book of Acts.

> Then some of the itinerant Jewish exorcists took it upon themselves to **call**

the name of the Lord Jesus over those who
had **evil spirits**, saying, "We exorcise
you by the Jesus whom Paul preaches."
Also there were seven sons of Sceva, a
Jewish chief priest, who did so. And the
evil spirit answered and said, "Jesus I
know, and Paul I know; but who are
you?" Then the man in whom the evil
spirit was leaped on them, overpowered
them, and prevailed against them, so
that they fled out of that house naked
and wounded. This became known
both to all Jews and Greeks dwelling in
Ephesus; and fear fell on them all, and
the name of the Lord Jesus was magni-
fied (Acts 19:13-17).

It is clear that to cast out a devil, it's not enough to have
the name only—you have to know the One who bore the
name. Now you say, "Who are these people?" Look again
at the account of the last days in Matthew 24.

"Then **many false prophets** will rise up
and **deceive many**." And because **lawlessness will abound**, the **love** of **many** will grow
cold (Matthew 24:11-12).

"The **love** of many will grow cold!" The Greek word
for "love" in this verse is *agape*. *Agape* is the God kind of
love. It is the love that describes God's love for us. There
are several Greek words translated "love" in the New
Testament. Jesus introduced *agape* and said it would be
shed abroad in the hearts of those who receive Him. The
world or non-Christians would not know this kind of

love. So the many who are deceived by these false prophets are not heathens.

Why would the love of God in them grow cold? The answer is "because lawlessness [iniquity, KJV] will abound." What will Jesus say to the many who come to Him on judgment day? "And then I will declare to them, 'I never knew you; depart from Me, you who **practice lawlessness!**'"

One day God gave me a very sobering vision. I saw *many*, not a few and not even *some* but *many*, coming to the gates of pearl, fully expecting to hear Jesus say, "Enter into the joy of the Lord." Instead they heard the words, "I never knew you; depart from Me!" What a tragedy! People who were so deceived that they called Him "Lord" and did miracles in His name still were denied entrance to the kingdom of heaven. He was talking about people who attended churches that believe in the gifts of the Spirit, who called themselves "full gospel!"

You may now be thinking, "But Jesus said He had never known them; therefore, how could they have cast out devils and done miracles in His name? How can this be?"

There are two possible groups of people. The first are those who joined themselves with Jesus for the benefits of salvation out of selfish motives. They never came to know the heart of God; they only wanted His power and blessings. They sought Him for their own benefit, so their service for Him was entirely self-motivated, not love-motivated. First Corinthians 8:3 says, "But if anyone **loves God**, this one is **known by Him**." Remember Jesus said, "I never knew you." So the one who does not love God is not known by God. There are those who say they love God but do not. This lack of love is confirmed by their actions even though they boldly confess it.

Loving God means you lay your life down for Him. You no longer live for yourself but for Him.

Judas sought Jesus and joined himself with Jesus. It appeared he loved God by the great sacrifice he made to follow Him. Judas left all to join the ministry team and go on the road with Jesus. Judas stayed even under the heat of persecution; he didn't quit. He cast out devils, healed the sick, and preached the gospel. We have no record it was any other way. However, Judas' intentions were not right from the start. He never repented of his self-seeking motives. His character was revealed by statements such as: "What are you willing **to give me** if I . . ." (Matthew 26:14). He lied and flattered to gain advantage (Matthew 26:25), he took money from the treasury of Jesus' ministry for personal use (John 12:4-6), and the list goes on. He never knew the Lord even though he spent three and a half years in His company!

There are those not unlike Judas who make great sacrifices for the ministry, even casting out devils, healing the sick, and preaching the gospel, but they have never known Him for it was all done out of selfish motives, not for the love of God.

The second possibility of those who hear the Master say, "Depart from Me, you who practice lawlessness!" are men or women who, because of sin abounding in their lives (Matthew 24:11-12), slid back permanently from following Jesus. The love of God grew cold in them because of their continued practice of sin or iniquity. Look at what God says through the prophet Ezekiel.

> "But when a righteous man **turns away**
> **from his righteousness and commits iniquity**,
> and does according to all the abomina-

tions that the wicked man does, shall he live? All the righteousness which he has done shall **not be remembered**; because of the unfaithfulness of which he is guilty and the sin which he has committed, because of them he shall **die**" (Ezekiel 18:24).

God says He will not remember his righteousness. When God forgets something, it is as if it never happened. We speak about God forgetting our sin, burying it in the sea of forgetfulness. God will not remember our sins anymore. The devil tries to accuse us, but God said He will remember them no more. So in His mind it is as though we have never sinned. Well, the converse is also true. When God says a man's righteousness will not be remembered, He means He will forget He once knew him. That is why Jesus will say, "I never knew you."

ONCE SAVED—ALWAYS SAVED?

A very deceptive doctrine has been propagated throughout the Church that once a person is saved there is no way he can ever lose his salvation. Let's examine this with Old and New Testament scriptures.

Brethren, if anyone among you WANDERS from the truth, and someone turns him back, let him know that he who **turns a sinner** from the error of his way will **save a soul from death** and cover a multitude of sins (James 5:19-20).

The first thing we must notice is that James says, **"Brethren,** if anyone among **you** . . . ." He is not talking to people who just think they are Christians. He is speaking of a believer who wanders from the way of truth. Notice that James specifically calls a brother that wanders from the truth a sinner. The result, if there is no **turning back to God (repentance), is death.** The book of Proverbs amplifies this by saying:

> A man who **wanders** from the way of understanding will **rest in the assembly of the dead** (Proverbs 21:16).

Proverbs says the place of rest or final home of a man or woman who wanders from the truth of the gospel without turning back to the way of righteousness is the assembly of the dead, which is Hades or hell. Again Peter makes it plain:

> For if, after they have escaped the pollutions of the world through the **knowledge of the Lord and Savior Jesus Christ,** they are **again entangled** in them and **overcome,** the latter end is worse for them than the beginning. **For it would have been better for them not to have known the way of righteousness, than having known it, to turn from the holy commandment delivered to them.** But it has happened to them according to the true proverb: "A dog returns to his own vomit," and, "a sow, having washed, to her wallowing in the mire" (2 Peter 2:20-22).

Peter describes those who have escaped the pollutions of the world through the knowledge of Jesus Christ but are again entangled in the ways of the world and overcome by it. To be overcome by it means they did not return to the Lord. They did not repent of their lawlessness. Peter states it would have been better for them never to have known the **way of righteousness** than to have known it and turned from the way of the Lord. In other words, God is saying it is better never to have gotten saved than to receive the gift of eternal life and then turn from it permanently. This goes closely in line with what Ezekiel said: "All the **righteousness** which he has done shall **not be remembered**."

Why would it have been better to have never known the way of righteousness? Jude answers this by saying, ". . . for whom is reserved the **blackness** of darkness forever . . ." (Jude 13). The blackness of darkness means a worse punishment. ". . . That servant who knew his master's will, and **did not prepare himself or do according to his will**, shall be beaten with **many stripes**. But he who did not know, yet committed things deserving of stripes, shall be beaten with few" (Luke 12:47-48). In Jude's account of this greater punishment, he was speaking of those who are "**twice dead**" (Jude 12-13). To be twice dead means you were once dead without Christ, then you were made alive by receiving Him, then you died again by departing from Him permanently.

There are many other scriptures in the New Testament to support this. Many people are deceived into thinking they can live their lives the way they want to and just confess Jesus as Savior and still be saved. They have pulled scriptures out of the Bible that support their doctrine, such as God saying, "I will never leave you nor forsake you" (Hebrews 13:6). God will not leave us, but He never said we could not leave Him. Second Timothy 2:12 says, "If we deny Him, He also will deny us." A person can deny Christ not only by his/her words but also by his/her actions! In fact, actions speak louder than words. Titus 1:16 says, "They **profess** to know God, but in works they deny Him." Titus makes it clear that a person can profess or confess to know Jesus Christ, but by their **works they deny Him**.

James said it this way: "What does it profit, my brethren, if someone **says** he has faith but **does not have works?** Can faith save him?" (James 2:14). Can just saying you believe in Jesus Christ and praying a sinner's prayer at some time in your life save you even if there are no corresponding actions to back up your words? James went on to say, "Show me your faith without your works and I will show you my faith by my works" (verse 18). He was saying, "My works (actions) will speak louder than my words!" So it goes right back to what Jesus said: "You will know them by their fruits [not by their words!]" (Matthew 7:15). What is the fruit of their lives? Are they motivated by selfish ambition? Are they living for themselves? Have they laid down their lives to follow Jesus?

Some have been shaken by this message God has told me to preach. They come to me in a panicked state, saying, "I thought once saved you were always saved!" My response to them is, "If you truly love Jesus Christ, you will not deny Him in thoughts, words, or actions!"

John says, "My little children, these things I write to you, so that **you may not sin. And if anyone sins**, we have an Advocate with the Father, Jesus Christ the righteous (1 John 2:1). The aim of those who love God is not to sin, but if he does sin he has an advocate with the Father,

Jesus Christ the righteous, and he can confess his sin to the righteous Advocate and be forgiven. He did not say, "My little children, these things I write to you, so that **you may sin. And when you sin you** have an Advocate with the Father, Jesus Christ the righteous." (Compare the two statements in bold carefully!)

Jude warned us by the Spirit of God that men and women would creep into the Church turning the grace of God into a means of fulfilling selfish desires and deny the Lord Jesus Christ with their covetous and rebellious ways. He began his letter with, "Beloved, while I was very diligent to write to you concerning our common salvation, I found it necessary to write to you exhorting you to **contend earnestly for the faith.**" How do we contend or fight to keep the faith? He answers, "But you, beloved, building yourselves up on your most holy faith, praying in the Holy Spirit, **keep yourselves in the love of God . . .**" (verses 20-21). Don't allow your love to grow cold through the deceitfulness of sin. You contend for the faith by protecting your love for God even when men or women in your midst profess Christianity but live a lifestyle of covetousness and rebellion. *Don't allow their leaven of hypocrisy to filter into your heart and mind!*

If Jude commands us to keep ourselves in the love of God, that means love can be lost. These are the second group who will hear the master say "Depart . . . ."

If you love God, you will have no trouble keeping His commandments! If serving God is an obligation, you have entered into a legalistic relationship, and it will be hard to keep His commandments. We should not serve God to earn His approval; we should serve God because we are in love with Him! Jude goes on to tell us how to keep that love fresh even if there is bad leaven in the Church. He says, "Keep yourselves in the love of God,

looking for the mercy of our Lord Jesus Christ unto eternal life" (Jude 21). We are to look for the Lord every moment of the day. We are to long for Him and seek Him continually that He might reveal Himself in a greater way. For "... everyone who has this hope in Him [the hope of Jesus revealing Himself] **purifies** himself, just as He is pure" (1 John 3:3).

"Blessed are those servants whom the master, when he comes, will find **watching**. But if that **servant says in his heart, 'My master** is delaying his coming,' and begins to beat the male and female servants, and to eat and drink and be drunk, the master of that servant will come on a day when he is not **looking** for him, and at an hour when he is not aware, and will cut him in two and appoint him his portion with the **unbelievers**. And that servant who **knew his master's will** and did not prepare himself or do according to his will, shall be beaten with many stripes. But he who did not know, yet committed things deserving of stripes, shall be beaten with few" (Luke 12:37-48).

At the conclusion of the book of Jude is one of my favorite promises in the Bible. To those who keep themselves in love with God by looking for the revealing of Jesus He says:

Now to Him who is able to keep you from stumbling, and to present you faultless before the presence of His glory with exceeding joy, to God our Savior, who alone is wise, be glory and majesty, dominion and power, both now and forever. Amen (Jude 24-25).

God will keep us from stumbling and present us faultless before the presence of His glory with exceeding joy! This comforts the hearts of those who are sincere but get shaken about the discussion of "once saved always saved." I exhort them, "If you love God and pursue Him, He will keep you blameless!" Those who truly serve Him will not fall short because of the grace of God.

TRUE OR FALSE REPENTANCE?

He is calling us to repent of the nature that breeds sin.

"Not everyone who says to Me, 'Lord, Lord,' shall enter the kingdom of heaven, but he who does the will of My Father in heaven. Many will say to Me in that day, 'Lord, Lord, have we not prophesied in Your name, cast out demons in Your name, and done many wonders in Your name?' And then I will declare to them, 'I never knew you; depart from Me, you who **practice lawlessness!**'"

Matthew 7:21-23

PRACTICING SIN

Notice Jesus said, "I never knew you; depart from me you who **practice** lawlessness!" The key word in this statement is practice. First John 3:4-8 says, "Whoever commits sin also commits lawlessness, and sin is lawlessness. . . . Little children, let no one deceive you. He

79

who **practices** righteousness is righteous, just as He is righteous. He who sins **[practices lawlessness]** is of the devil . . . ."
Now read carefully what the works of the flesh are in the following verses. Notice the word *practice*.

Now the **works of the flesh** are evident, which are: adultery, fornication, uncleanness, lewdness [excess or unbridled lust], idolatry, sorcery, hatred, contentions, jealousies, outbursts of wrath, selfish ambitions, dissensions, heresies, envy, murders, drunkenness, revelries, and the like; of which I tell you beforehand, just as I also told you in time past, that those who **practice** such things **will not inherit the kingdom of God** (Galations 5:19-21).

At this point let's define the word "practice." A few definitions are "to do frequently or as a rule; to perform often in order to learn; to teach by frequent repetition; to do something habitually." The person who "practices sin" is the person who sins without conviction, even if it is only one time a week or a couple of times a month, and says something like this to justify it, "Oh well, it is only weakness. I am better than most of the Christians in my Church. If God forgave those people He will surely forgive me because, after all, nobody is perfect, and I am far better than them." There is no genuine repentance. He is not sorry he has hurt the heart of God.

In the Church we categorize sin. We place sins like drunkenness, adultery, and homosexuality in one category, and sins of hatred, gossip, strife, and others like them in a different category. We have decided that people who are in the first category (drunkenness, adultery, homosexuality) are in danger of hell, but those in the second category of sin (hatred, gossip, pride, etc.) are just weak. This is a self-righteous, religious lie. God does not categorize sin but puts them all in the same category. He declares that all who practice such things will not inherit the kingdom of God! God sandwiches hatred, jealousy, outbursts of wrath, selfish ambitions, and envy between adultery and murder. If people knew that God viewed hatred and selfish ambitions, on the same basis as adultery and murder, they would not be so quick to yield to or excuse these sins! This tolerance for and practice of sin by men and women professing to be Christians has birthed deception.

This mind-set has caused the Church to become hard and judgmental. They look at those bound to homosexuality, alcohol, and drug addiction and judge them, while winking at the sins of unforgiveness, strife, gossip, and pride. Their hearts have grown insensitive to the conviction of the Holy Spirit.

Shortly after I was saved, my wife and I were discussing the woman who brought the alabaster flask of fragrant oil to the Pharisee's house and washed Jesus' feet with tears and anointed His feet with oil. As the woman did this, the Pharisee looked at her with contempt and thought that if Jesus were truly a prophet, He would not allow this harlot to do this. Jesus looked at Simon the Pharisee and said, "There was a certain creditor who had two debtors. One owed five hundred denarii, and the other fifty. And when they had nothing with which to repay, he freely forgave them both. Tell Me, therefore, **which of them will love him more?**" Simon answered by saying the one who was forgiven of the five hundred denarii would love more since he was forgiven of the most. Jesus responded, saying that Simon had judged rightly!

I told my wife, "Sometimes I wish I had been a drug dealer, a thief, or some other kind of wicked criminal before I met Jesus; then I would love Him more because I was forgiven more. I want to love Him as much as possible!" As we further discussed this, the Lord said to me, "John, you don't understand what I was saying. I was dealing with the attitude of Simon's heart. He saw this woman as one type of sinner and himself as another, much better person, only requiring a little forgiveness. I said, 'Whoever shall keep the whole law, and yet stumble in one point, he is guilty of all' (James 2:10-11). In My eyes the person who tells only one lie all their life is the same as the worst prisoner! The destination of both is the same if they are not saved!"

I felt a release of life as I realized I could love Him as much as anyone else, because I had been under the same judgment as the worst criminal on death row!

The problem is, our society, encouraged by religion, categorizes sinners. So those considered "good people" are under the deception that they need only a little grace. A few months ago, a man from Alabama phoned me. I had been to a church in his city, and he had attended the meetings and was ministered to. I knew when I was at the meetings that he was a homosexual. A few weeks later he called and told me he was a homosexual, and I told him I already had known that. His voice became defensive. "You probably saw me as some weird pervert, right?" My immediate response was, "No!" I began to apologize for what many of us Christians have done. I said, "Please forgive us for placing homosexuality in one category of sin and everything else in another. I was bound by sin and heading to the same hell as you were.

My need for a Savior was just as great. My own sins
were just more socially acceptable. However, they were
just as great an offense to God." He saw my heart, and
we prayed together. God delivered him. A few months
later he called and relayed with great excitement what
Jesus was doing in his life. Praise God!

We must realize that sin is sin, no matter what the
type. Those who **tolerate any sin** are in danger of hearing
the master say, "Depart . . . ."

SORROW OF THE WORLD,
OR GODLY SORROW?

> Now I rejoice, not that you were made
> sorry, but that your sorrow led to **repen-**
> **tance.** For you were made sorry in a godly
> manner, that you might suffer loss from
> us in nothing. For **godly sorrow** produces
> repentance leading to salvation, not to be
> regretted; but the **sorrow of the world** pro-
> duces death (2 Corinthians 7:9-10).

Paul is writing this to the Church, not the world.
Repentance is for the world as well as the Church. In
the above verse, "repentance" is from the Greek word
metanoia meaning "a change of mind." God is not
looking for repentance of sins only but for a change of
mind and heart toward the thought processes that tolerate this way of life. He wants us to repent of the character that breeds sin.

Repentance is more than apologizing for something we have done. Paul said that there is a sorrow
that does not produce repentance, but rather death!

Not all sorrow is godly. Not all tears are motivated by genuine repentance. In fact, they may be shed without genuine repentance.

From the above verse we see there is a type of sorrow (of the world) that will lead to death and another type (godly sorrow) that leads to life. What is this difference between "godly and worldly sorrow"? The difference is simple: sorrow of the world focuses on you, while godly sorrow focuses on Jesus. Sorrow of the world is concerned *about the consequences* resulting from sin, not that sin has separated a person from the heart of God. When a person is concerned about how his sin affects his status, welfare, position, or reputation, it is not godly sorrow. This bears a selfish focus which leads that person deeper into a hardened state of heart! This eventually leads to death!

To illustrate the difference, we will examine the lives and motives of King Saul and King David. God commanded King Saul in 1 Samuel 15 to attack Amalek and to utterly destroy all they had. He was to kill man, woman, child and nursing infant, their ox, sheep, camels, and donkeys. Saul went to war; however, he took the king alive and spared the best of the sheep, oxen, fatlings, lambs, and all that was good, unwilling to utterly destroy them. Then the word of the Lord came to the prophet Samuel how Saul had disobeyed the commandment of the Lord. Samuel confronted Saul because there was no conviction in Saul's own heart. Saul defended himself, claiming he had done all God had commanded of him. Samuel pointed out specifically what Saul had omitted, and when Saul saw Samuel was correct, he excused himself and blamed the people. Samuel declared it was he who had disobeyed the commandment of the Lord. When Saul realized there was no one left to blame, he responded: "**I have sinned; yet honor me now, please, before the elders of my people and before Israel,** and return with me, that I may worship the Lord your God" (1 Samuel 15:30). He acknowledged his sin as many do when they are caught with their backs to the wall. However, it was worldly sorrow, for he was concerned about this exposé in front of his elders and the men of Israel, not that he had sinned against God. His response was to guard his reputation and kingdom. His motive: selfish ambition. As a result, the kingdom he tried so hard to protect **his own way** was torn from him. He feared man more than he feared God, which is the case of those whose motive is self-seeking!

Now look at King David. David committed adultery with Bathsheba, wife of Uriah the Hittite, David's faithful servant. When David found out she was pregnant as a result of this liaison, and her husband would not go to be with her when his men were on the battlefield, David put Uriah on the front lines with an order to Joab to draw back so the enemy could kill him. David committed adultery and premeditated a murder to cover his sin. Then he was confronted by the prophet Nathan. When his sin was exposed, "David said to Nathan, '**I have sinned against the Lord**' (2 Samuel 12:13). Both Saul and David confessed they had sinned, yet David understood who his sin was against and fell on his face in repentance. David was not concerned with what his elders or the men of Israel might think; he only cared what God thought. He knew he had hurt God's heart. He cried out: "Against You, You only, have I sinned, and done this evil in Your sight . . ." (Psalm 51:4). David was a man after God's heart, while Saul was after a kingdom! David was sustained by his love for God; Saul was destroyed by his love for self.

As a teenager I became bound to the sin of sexual lust. The majority of American males are also bound to lust. This didn't just leave when I accepted Jesus Christ but stayed to torment me. Time and time again I would cry out to God, begging His forgiveness. I thought when I got married it would leave, but sadly, I discovered it did not. It hindered a normal sexual relationship with my wife, whom I loved so much. I was tormented by this sin. I was bound!

In 1984 I approached a well-known minister and confessed this sin. He was known as one of the most powerful ministers in America. I thought if anyone could get me free, he could. He looked at me and said, "If you only knew how many men in the Church and in ministry are bound to this same thing." He began to talk with me a few minutes, and then I said, "Please pray for me that I might be free." So he did, but nothing happened. I knew the problem wasn't him, so I couldn't figure out why I wasn't free.

One year later, May 2, 1985, I went away on a four-day fast. I was fed up with this sin. I knew it hurt God, and that Jesus had already paid the price for me to be free. On the fourth day of that fast, God led me in a deliverance prayer, and the spirit of lust left me! I was free! And I'm still free today!

When I inquired of the Lord why He hadn't set me free a year earlier when I was prayed for by that minister, he showed that my initial sorrow was after a worldly manner. I wanted to be free because I thought if I didn't get rid of this sin, God wouldn't promote me from the ministry of helps into a preaching ministry. I was more concerned about the consequences of this sin and how it would affect my ministry than the fact I was sinning against God. Yet, a year later my sorrow had changed, and now my motive was not fear of consequences on my ministry, but that I loved God and wanted nothing between us. Godly sorrow produced life-yielding repentance which led to salvation (2 Corinthians 7:10). "Salvation" in that verse is from the Greek word *sozo* which from Strong's Greek dictionary is defined: "healing, preservation, wholeness, soundness, and deliverance." So my godly sorrow produced repentance, which granted deliverance!

REPENTANCE IS THE PREREQUISITE TO DELIVERANCE

In the Church many want deliverance without realizing repentance is a prerequisite. Watch this account of Jesus sending out the twelve disciples:

> And He called the twelve to Himself,
> and began to send them out two by two,
> and **gave them power over unclean spirits. . . .**
> So they went out and preached that people **should repent**. And they **cast out many demons** . . . (Mark 6:7-12).

Jesus outlined repentance as creating an atmosphere for deliverance. There are those who have come to me in prayer lines and in private, wanting to be free of the torment of some particular sin, but they are unwilling to change their attitude toward this sin. They enjoy the sin but do not like the consequences or guilt they experience afterward. If there were a way they could remain Christians and stay involved in their sins, they would do it because they still enjoy it!

Before entering the ministry, a pastor friend of mine from Southern California was bound to cigarettes. He smoked two packs a day and wanted to be free. He had begged God for two and a half years to be free. One of his friends had gotten saved in a meeting and was instantly delivered from cigarettes. He saw this and became very upset with God. Why had God so quickly delivered his friend when he had been believing for two and a half years to be free? He left the meeting in a rage and went home and complained to God. After complaining for several minutes, he blurted out, "Why did you deliver my friend and not me?" The Lord replied, "Because you still like it!" He said he took one look at the lit cigarette in his hand and put it out. He was free and never picked up another cigarette!

As long as you like your sin, you will not be free from it. You must learn to hate sin as God does. You say, "How do I learn to hate something my flesh enjoys?" First realize sin is what nailed Jesus Christ to the cross. First Peter 2:24 says, "Who Himself bore our sins in His own body on the tree . . . ." The next thing to realize is that sin will sever your fellowship with God. Isaiah 59:2 says, "But your iniquities have separated you from your God; and your sins have hidden His face from you, so that He will not hear." The third thing to realize is that sin is candy-coated arsenic. Romans 8:12-13 says, "Therefore, **brethren**, we are debtors—not to the flesh, to live according to the flesh. For **if you live according to the flesh you will die** . . . ." Notice Paul was addressing "brethren," not unbelievers. He warns of the tragic result of living in the flesh and tolerating sin. Sin may be enjoyable for a season, but in the end it always produces death. We see Moses "choosing rather to suffer affliction with the people of God than to **enjoy the passing [temporary] pleasures of**

sin" (Hebrews 11:25). Sin is pleasurable to the flesh, but its pleasure lasts only a short season.

A woman called me and confessed she had gotten into an adulterous relationship with another "Christian" man. She said her husband was not a Christian and was verbally abusive to her about her faith. She said that she had repented of her sin. She then told me her "Christian" friends counseled her to divorce her husband and marry this nice "Christian" man who loved her. She wasn't sure they were right and wanted my opinion. I could tell it wouldn't take much to persuade her to leave her husband and marry this other man. She knew in her heart it was wrong, but she was looking for permission to go ahead and do it. It is important we always tell the truth, even when it is not what people want to hear. First I said that she had not repented. She said, "But I have repented with tears." I then said, "You don't hate this sin; you just know it is wrong and will not be blessed. You still like it." She said, "I don't get what you are saying. I did repent."

Her idea of repentance was acknowledgment that the act of adultery was wrong. Remember, God is looking for more. He wants a change of heart and mind. He is calling us to repent of the nature that breeds sin. If she didn't genuinely repent of her heart attitude toward this man, it would eventually lead to divorce in order to get what she wanted from the start. So I said to her, "Suppose someone told you, 'There is going to be a sexual orgy down the street. Would you like to go?' How would you respond to that?" She was repulsed by what I said and replied, "I wouldn't want anything to do with that." I said, "When you can look at the adulterous affair with this 'Christian' man the way you just responded to that orgy, then you will have come to the place where you have truly repented!" She finally understood.

THE FRUIT OF REPENTANCE

Therefore **bear fruits worthy of repentance** . . . (Luke 3:8-9).

How many times have we seen men and women hear a message and, under conviction of the Spirit, respond to a call by the minister and pray a prayer of repentance at the altar, but the work of repentance is not done because no fruit is brought forth? They are temporarily relieved by the prayer but soon return to the original life-style. Repentance is not a one-time prayer of relief but a way of life! It is a decision from your heart to change. The work of repentance is not complete until the fruit of righteousness appears. The prayer of repentance is only the beginning.

Paul wrote to the Corinthian Church in his first letter and rebuked them for their carnality. He wrote a very convicting letter, which brought repentance! In his follow-up letter he acknowledged they had sorrowed in a godly manner, which produced repentance. Now let's look at the fruit it produced.

For godly sorrow produces repentance leading to salvation, not to be regretted; but the sorrow of the world produces death. For observe this very thing, that you sorrowed in a godly manner: What **diligence** it produced in you, what **clearing** of yourselves, what **indignation**, what **fear**, what **vehement desire**, what **zeal**, what **vindication**! In all

things you proved yourselves to be clear in
this matter (2 Corinthians 7:10-11).

Notice he lists seven fruits of repentance. These are
characteristics of a believer who is on fire, not lukewarm.
People wonder why some Christians are so diligent and
zealous. The reason: they have nothing in their hearts to
distract them from their purpose. Often we try to live in
both worlds. The world of the flesh cools the fire of the
world of the spirit. Let's briefly study all seven fruits.

1. Diligence – When the heart is focused, you will be
   diligent. We are told, "He who comes to God must
   believe that He is, and that He is a rewarder of
   those who **diligently** seek Him" (Hebrews 11:6). If
   you vacillate back and forth, living in the natural
   world and the spirit world, you will be slothful
   spiritually. We are commanded to be ". . . not lag-
   ging in **diligence**, fervent in spirit, serving the
   Lord" (Romans 12:11).

2. Clearing of yourselves – Many live under the weight
   of guilt. Jesus came to set us free from the guilt of
   sin. If repentance is genuine it produces a clearing
   of your conscience that is produced no other way.

3. Indignation – Repentance will produce a hatred of
   sin. God the Father said to Jesus, "You have loved
   righteousness and **hated lawlessness**; therefore
   God, Your God, has **anointed** You with the oil of
   gladness more than Your companions" (Hebrews
   1:9). Many love righteousness but do not hate sin.
   The anointing is therefore weak. When you hate
   sin, you will see an increase in the anointing on
   your life.

4. Fear – An entire book could be written on this. We are told holiness is perfected in the fear of the Lord (2 Corinthians 7:1), because "the fear of the Lord is to hate evil; pride and arrogance and the evil way . . ." and "the fear of the Lord is the beginning of wisdom . . ." (Proverbs 8:13; 9:10).

5. Vehement desire – Desire is the drive or life behind prayer, creating a climate to receive from God. Jesus said, "Therefore I say unto you, 'What things soever ye **desire**, when ye pray, believe that ye receive them, and ye shall have them'" (Mark 11:24, KJV). If your prayer time is lifeless, it is because your desire is not strong. Repentance will produce vehement desire!

6. Zeal – The dictionary defines this word as "to be eager or enthusiastic." When Jesus ran the money changers from the temple, His disciples remembered it was written, "Zeal for Your house has eaten Me up" (John 2:13-17). Jesus commanded the lukewarm Church to "be zealous and repent" (Revelation 3:19).

7. Vindication – The dictionary defines this word as "to lay claim to, avenge." The Bible says in James 4:7, "Therefore submit to God. Resist the devil and he will flee from you." The way to resist the devil is to submit to God! This is perfect vindication. Your greatest weapon against the devil is not your mouth but your humility and holy life-style!

Repentance will produce these godly qualities, which are the fruit Jesus commanded us to produce. We cannot imitate these characteristics. They only come forth from a pure heart.

God is calling His children to a holy life. People who tolerate sin will not see God, for He has said we are to "Pursue . . . holiness, without which no one will see the Lord" (Hebrews 12:14). Holiness is a work of His grace, not a work of the flesh. This work begins in our heart through the avenue of repentance. Many have tried to live holy life-styles in their own strength and ended up in the bondage of legalism. The way to holiness is by humbling ourselves in repentance. For He gives grace to the humble, and grace is what enables us to walk in what truth requires.

8 ▼ THE GOSPEL OF SELF

Our message is "Come to Jesus and get . . ."

"But why do you **call Me 'Lord, Lord,'**
and do not do the things which I say?"
Luke 6:46

COME TO JESUS AND GET . . .

"Not everyone who says to Me, 'Lord, Lord,' shall enter the kingdom of heaven, but he who does the will of My Father in heaven. Many will say to Me in that day, 'Lord, Lord . . .'" (Matthew 7:21-22). Many today call Him Lord, professing to be born-again Christians, attending church regularly, and possibly speaking in other tongues, but is He their Lord? It is one thing to call Him Lord but another to live a life in submission to His Lordship! As James boldly put it, "Show me your faith without your works, and I will show you my faith by my works" (James 2:18).

The word "Lord" in the above verse comes from the Greek word *kurios*. Strong's dictionary of Greek words

defines this word as "supreme in authority or master."
Jesus was saying there will be men and women who confess with their mouths that He is supreme in authority, but
they live lives that do not bear up what they say. For this
reason Jesus said, "But why do you call Me 'Lord, Lord,'
and do not do the things which I say?" (Luke 6:46).

In America and in other parts of the world many
have preached Jesus as Savior only! We've done anything to fill the altar with "converts" and our churches
with tithing members. Our message is, "Come to Jesus
and get . . . salvation, peace, love, joy, prosperity, success, health, etc." We have cheapened the gospel to a
solution to life's problems or an improvement of your
life-style. We have enticed sinners by preaching only
the blessings to be obtained in following Him. Jesus has
been sold by salesmen trying to meet their quota! To
do this we have bypassed repentance to gain a "convert." So converts we have. But what kind? In describing the ministers of His day, Jesus said, "You travel
over land and sea to win a single **convert,** and when he
becomes one, you make him twice as much a son of
hell as you are" (Matthew 23:15, NIV). Converts are
easily made, but are they truly sons of the kingdom of
God? Self-seeking converts, not disciples, are spawned
by what we have lived and preached. We have not boldly proclaimed the price to follow Him—at least not as
loudly as we have the benefits!

Jesus made it clear to the multitudes, "Whoever
desires to come after Me, let him **deny himself, and take
up his cross,** and follow Me. For whoever **desires** to save
his life will lose it, but whoever loses his life for My sake
and the gospel's will save it" (Mark 8:34-35). Notice
He does *not* say, "Whoever **desires** to lose his life for My
sake . . . will save it." Just desiring to lose your life is not

enough. There are many not attending church who would gladly receive the benefits of salvation if only they could keep their own lives too. They realize there is a price that they are not ready to pay to serve God. They are honest with God and themselves. Yet, there are hypocrites who attend church, call Him, Lord, declare their submission to His Lordship but have hidden idols in their heart. They love these more than God, and they live the life of a hypocrite.

The result of this "come to Jesus and get . . ." gospel are converts who merely desire an improved lifestyle and who don't want to go to hell. They receive Him as the Savior who blesses—but not as Lord.

AN UN-AMERICAN GOSPEL

We do not see this in the ministry of Jesus. His message was very different from what has been preached in America! Watch how Jesus handled one young man.

> Now as He was going out on the road, **one came running, knelt** before Him, and asked Him, "Good Teacher, what shall I do that I may inherit eternal life?" (Mark 10:17).

The first thing I want you to notice is that, this man came **running** after Jesus. When he arrived, he **knelt** before Jesus and asked what he needed to do to get saved. I can just see this man running through the crowd around Jesus, kneeling, grabbing His arm, and with great passion pleading, "What shall I do to be saved?" To date, neither in my personal life or ministry, have I had **any** person, rich or poor, run to me, kneel down, and plead, "What do I do to get born again?" This man was intense! Some may picture this wealthy young ruler casually sauntering up to Jesus with a cool, reserved, intellectual tone in his voice, calmly asking what a person must do to inherit eternal life. This was not at all the case. This man was serious about getting saved! Watch!

> "**Good Teacher,** what shall I do that I may inherit eternal life?" So Jesus said to him, "Why do you call Me good? No one is good but One, that is, God" (Mark 10:17-18).

He was not flattering Jesus, he did not call Jesus "Good Lord." I believe this man had integrity. He knew that to call Jesus Lord he would need to do what He said! Many Christians today don't have this much character. They call Jesus Lord and say their pastor is the leader, yet they will not do what the Lord asks of them or receive instruction from their pastor. They smile, say "amen" to what the pastor preaches, but don't apply it to their own life. They have ears to hear but do not apply what the Spirit is saying to them. Many times they feel the message is appropriate for others they consider "worse off than themselves." They are hypocrites! They try to remove specks in their brothers' eyes while a log blinds their own.

Now hear how Jesus ministers to this intense man, wanting to get saved.

> "You know the commandments: 'Do not commit adultery,' 'Do not murder,' 'Do not steal,' 'Do not bear false witness,'

'Do not defraud,' 'Honor your father and
your mother.'" And he answered and said
to Him, "Teacher, all these things I have
kept from my youth" (Mark 10:19-20).

Jesus quoted the last six of the Ten Commandments,
all of which deal with man's relationship with each other.
The young man eagerly replied that he had kept them all
from his youth. I believe this man did keep them. We see
his heart in approaching Jesus. However, Jesus purpose-
ly omitted the first four commandments. These deal
with a man's relationship with God—the first, to have no
other gods or idols **before** God. In other words, nothing
in our lives should come before our affection, love, and
commitment to God. This young man had not fulfilled
these commandments, nor at that moment was he willing to; Jesus had exposed idols in his life.

Then Jesus, looking at him, **loved him**,
and said to him, "**One thing you lack**: Go
your way, sell whatever you have and give
to the poor, and you will have treasure in
heaven; and **come, take up the cross, and follow Me**" (Mark 10:21).

Notice, Jesus loved him! But how did He show his
love for this man? Was it by making the gospel a little
easier in case He might offend him? Was it by not confronting the idols of position, power, and money in his
life? Why didn't He just have him pray the sinner's
prayer, hoping he would forsake these idols at a later
date. After all, he was a prime candidate, with his
great intensity to be saved. All Jesus had to do was
draw the net and He would have had a wealthy, promi-

nent Christian! But Jesus loved him. Instead He gave this man truth—a very strong word, running the risk of losing this excited, powerful man. Jesus looked in his eyes and told him he lacked something, and what he lacked was not zeal, but the readiness of heart and mind to forsake all he had.

Can you imagine if Jesus told you there was something you lacked, and it would keep you from salvation! However, if you truly love, you are truthful, even if you know it means rejection. Many Christians and preachers flatter in fear of rejection from man. They want acceptance. I used to be like that. Everyone I met liked me, because I always told them what they wanted to hear. I hated confrontation and rejection and wanted everyone happy. Then God exposed my insecure, selfish motives. He revealed the focus of my love— myself, not the people who surrounded me. I was more concerned about their acceptance than giving them what was really needed.

It is much better to tell the truth than to compromise truth and have someone believe a lie. It is far better they hear it now than to believe they can keep sin in their lives and one day hear the Master say, "Depart; I never knew you. You were deceived!"

> But he was **sad** at this word, and **went away sorrowful**, for he had great possessions. Then Jesus looked around and said to His disciples, "How hard it is for those who have riches to enter the kingdom of God!" (Mark 10:22-23).

This man who was so eager now walks away sorrowful! "Oh, Jesus, how could You do that? The man came excited, and after hearing You preach he left *sad!* Don't You know you're supposed to end Your services on a high note? Your preaching should lift people and make them feel good about themselves, not sadden them. Your attendance will drop if you keep treating eager men and women like this, especially wealthy and influential ones. Go after him and soften it; surely he will come along after a while!"

That is what Jesus would hear today from His board members in America! Jesus would have been brought before them and His resignation requested. How dare He offend this potentially big tither! Doesn't He know they have a building program going on? I guess Jesus didn't understand the dynamics of building big, successful ministries, at least not like some ministers today have learned. Maybe He forgot for a moment how to win friends and influence people. Maybe He needed to tone down his sermons and preach nonconvicting messages. Messages which build self-esteem.

Doesn't this sound like America? We have fallen into the trap of doing anything to get a decision. Decisions are great as long as they are based on truth. The Lord showed me how many ministers, myself included, would have responded to this wealthy man running to me, kneeling, pleading, "Preacher, what do I do to get saved!" God showed me we'd say, "You want Jesus! You want to be a Christian! Praise the Lord, just pray this sinner's prayer with me. . . . Now, brother, come take up the checkbook and follow me and this gospel I preach!" We must realize God never called us to broaden the gospel, making it easier for people with idols to get "saved." Idols must be forsaken. Jesus must be received as Lord, not just Savior! Now watch what Jesus does after this wealthy man walks away.

Then Jesus looked around and said to His disciples, "How hard it is for those who have riches to enter the kingdom of God!" And the disciples were astonished at His words. But Jesus answered again and said to them, "Children, how **hard it is for those who trust in riches** to enter the kingdom of God! It is easier for a camel to go through the eye of a needle than for a rich man to enter the kingdom of God." And they were greatly astonished, saying among themselves, "Who then can be saved?" But Jesus looked at them and said, "With men it is impossible, but not with God; for with God all things are possible" (Mark 10:23-27).

He did not run after the man to bring him back. He turned to His staff and instructed them, "How hard it is for those who trust in riches . . . ." An idol is anything you love, trust in, or give your attention to before God! That man was unwilling to forsake his idol and follow Jesus. With some people, idols are popularity with their peers; with others it may be sports, food, television, or music. The list goes on. What may be an idol to one is not necessarily an idol to another. In Leviticus 26:1 God says, "You shall not make idols for yourselves." You are the one who makes it an idol, by loving or trusting it before God!

Notice also Jesus did not say, "Didn't I tell you if you obey the word the Father just gave Me for you, and give up this money, He will give you a hundredfold return!" Yet, we have done this. Ministers promise a hundredfold return from God in order to get people to respond to the word of the Lord. So the motive becomes, "Give in order to get!" If this was correct, then Jesus blew it. He should have focused in on the return rather than the cost. He did not try to entice this man into the kingdom by the blessings of the kingdom. Now watch in amazement what He goes on to say to Peter and the rest of the disciples.

> Then Peter began to say to Him, "See, we have **left all and followed You.**" So Jesus answered and said, "Assuredly, I say to you, there is no one who has left house or brothers or sisters or father or mother or wife or children or lands, for My sake and the gospel's, who shall not **receive a hundredfold now in this time**—houses and brothers and sisters and mothers and children and lands, with persecutions—and in the age to come, eternal life. But many who are first will be last, and the last first" (Mark 10:28-31).

Now Jesus looks at these who have already forsaken all to follow Him and says, "You will receive a hundred times as much in what you have given up now in this life, houses . . . and lands, with persecutions—and in the age to come, eternal life." If money had been Peter, James, John, and Andrew's motive for leaving and following Jesus, they would never have left their business. They were not aware of the hundredfold return promise. This was the first they heard it. They knew Jesus had the words of life and so left all—money was not an idol in their lives.

God has never demanded a person to be perfect in

order to follow Jesus. He has only asked for obedience to Him! This young ruler probably possessed characteristics much more polished than Peter. However, Peter was willing to do anything the Lord asked of him. That is what Jesus means when He calls us to forsake all to follow Him.

When I received Jesus Christ as Lord in 1979 and was filled with His Spirit, God immediately began dealing with me about the ministry. I was majoring in mechanical engineering at Purdue University and was on the dean's list, with plans to attend Harvard for an M.B.A. I wanted nothing to do with the ministry. All the ministers I had met were just men who I thought couldn't do much else in life. They all seemed weird. I had never met and spent time with a good minister. My other concept of ministry was living in Africa in a shack! But then the Spirit of God came on me during a service and said, "John, I have called you to preach. What are you going to do about it?" I thought, My family will disown me; they are all Catholic. I'll end up like all the other ministers. I don't really want to go to Africa. But I bowed my head and prayed, "Yes, Lord, I will obey You and preach no matter what the cost!" Now it has been nothing like what I thought, but God didn't show me that. He just wanted to know if I would forsake all to follow Him.

If you study the ministries of Peter, Paul, and the other disciples in the book of Acts and the epistles, you will see their messages lined up exactly with what Jesus preached to this wealthy man! Today we have deviated far from this path. It is the root reason for America's failing spiritual condition. We have made "born-again Christian" so easy to access that the way of truth has been grossly distorted. For this reason God is sending a call to His people to forsake their idols and turn back to the heart of God. To make ready a people for their Lord!

JOINED OR CONVERTED

"**Repent** therefore and be **converted, that your sins may be blotted out,** so that times of refreshing may come from the presence of the Lord, and that He may send Jesus Christ, who was preached to you before, whom heaven must receive until the times of restoration of all things, which God has spoken by the mouth of all His holy prophets since the world began" (Acts 3:19-21).

Peter boldly proclaimed this to the multitude who gathered, wanting to know what they should do to be saved after the healing of the crippled man at the temple. Repentance was the prerequisite to salvation. The first words out of the mouth of John the Baptist were, "**Repent,** for the kingdom of heaven is at hand!" (Matthew 3:2). The first words out of Jesus' mouth in His earthly ministry were, "**Repent,** for the kingdom of heaven is at hand" (Matthew 4:17). The first words out of Peter's mouth when the men and women wanted to know what to do to be saved on the day of Pentecost were, "**Repent,** and let every one of you be baptized in the name of Jesus Christ for the remission of sins . . ." (Acts 2:38). Paul, in describing his ministry to King Agrippa in the latter days of his life, said, "I was not disobedient to the heavenly vision, but declared first to those in Damascus and in Jerusalem, and throughout all the region of Judea, and then to the Gentiles, that they should **repent**, turn to God, and **do works befitting repentance**" (Acts 26:19).

First repentance, then conversion, for sins to be blotted out. A conversion is not genuine without repentance. It is a counterfeit conversion. This is not at all the gospel we've heard in the last part of the twentieth century. We have preached a message that will appeal to the desires of the humanity rather than proclaim the truth in love, which will bring repentance. We have turned the gospel into an invitation to a better life. However, the focus still remains on people's selfish desires. Repentance is not an option, it is a command. Acts 17:30 says, "Truly, these times of ignorance God overlooked, but now **commands** all men everywhere to **repent**" (Acts 17:30).

The Lord said to me one day, "Those who come to Me without repenting first are those who merely join themselves to Me." Conversion without repentance does not result in sins being blotted out! It just leads to more deception.

In a previous chapter we outlined how Judas sought Jesus and joined himself to Jesus. It appeared he loved God, for he made sacrifices to follow Him. He left all to join the ministry team and go on the road with Jesus. He stayed in the heat of persecution, cast out devils, healed the sick, and preached the gospel. However, Judas' intentions were not right from the start. He never repented of his self-seeking motives. He was deceived, and his deception grew worse until it ended in betraying Jesus!

The rich young ruler was honest. He counted the cost of denying himself, taking up the cross and following Jesus. He walked away but he knew the way of salvation.

The day may have come later, after Jesus was raised from the dead, that this man repented, especially since he had heard the truth in love!

There was an incident in the book of Acts where a man and his wife lied about an offering given. They sold a plot of land and kept back part of the proceeds. It was probably a very good piece of land worth a lot of money, and they did not want to part with it all. However, they wanted to be recognized as being big givers, so they told Peter in the presence of all that it was everything they received for the sale of the property. Peter confronted them both, and as a result of lying to the Spirit of God, they both fell over dead. The Bible says great fear came upon all the Church and upon all who heard these things. Yet look at this.

> And they were all with one accord in Solomon's Porch. Yet none of the rest dared **join** them, but the people esteemed them highly.
> And **believers were increasingly added to the Lord**, multitudes of both men and women (Acts 5:12-14).

None of the rest dared join them. Yet the next verse says believers were increasingly added to the Lord. It sounds like a contradiction. How could no one be joining them and yet believers be increasingly added to the Lord? What is being said here? It is simple: no one dared join themselves to Jesus without first repenting. Multitudes were **repenting** and being **converted** and were added to the Lord.

You may ask, "Why did this man and his wife fall over dead? There have been people who have lied to ministers since then and not fallen over dead." The reason can be found in the next verse.

> . . . so that they brought the sick out into the streets and laid them on beds and couches, that at least **the shadow of Peter** passing by might fall on some of them (Acts 5:15).

The glory of the Lord was manifesting so strong on Peter that just getting near him would drive out any manner of sickness or darkness. Ananias and Sapphira lied in the presence of the glory of the Lord. When you bring sin in contact with God's glory, there will be a reaction. Sin and anything that willfully bears it will be destroyed.

When the ark of God's presence was being brought back to Jerusalem by King David and his men, Uzzah put forth his hand to steady it at the threshing floor and was immediately struck dead! "The Lord's anger burned against Uzzah because of his irreverent act; therefore God struck him down and he died there beside the ark of God" (2 Samuel 6:7).

The reason God has not yet manifested His glory in the Church as strongly as He did in the book of Acts is because there would be many falling over dead, like this couple. So before the Lord comes in His glory to His temple (the Church), He will first send his messenger Elijah the prophet to call the people back to the heart of God (Malachi 3:1).

9 FLEE FROM IDOLATRY

"Idolatry": Excessive adoration or reverence of any person or thing.

> They feared the Lord, and served
> their own gods, after the manner of the
> nations . . .   2 Kings 17:33 (KJV)

THEY SERVE GOD AND THEIR IDOLS TOO

The NIV translation of the Bible says, "They worshipped the Lord, but they also served their own gods [idols] . . . ." Does this sound familiar? Don't men and women, young and old alike, "worship the Lord" in church, yet with idols in their hearts? Do Christians in this nation live any differently from those who do not profess to know Christ, as they serve their idols of the lusts of the flesh, the lusts of the eye, and the pride of life? How is this possible? Can a holy God have a Church full of idolatry? Is this the Church He is coming for? Absolutely not! He is returning for a holy Church, not one chasing what the world pursues! Look at Paul's address to the Corinthian Church.

Therefore, my dear friends, **flee from idolatry.** I speak to sensible people; judge for yourselves what I say. . . . Consider the people of Israel: Do not those who eat the sacrifices **participate** in the altar? Do I mean then that **a sacrifice offered to an idol is anything,** or that **an idol is anything?** No, but the sacrifices of pagans are offered to demons, not to God, and I do not want you to be **participants** with demons. You cannot drink the cup of the Lord and the cup of demons too; **you cannot have a part in both the Lord's table and the table of demons.** Are we trying to arouse the Lord's jealousy? Are we stronger than He? (1 Corinthians 10:14-22, NIV).

An idol in itself is nothing! The golden calf the children of Israel built in the desert while Moses was on the mountain had no power in itself. Its power lay in the hearts of the children of Israel. They gave their affections, love, and trust to it. So they built it an altar in their heart. When speaking of the children of Israel, God said, "She has never given up her harlotry [idolatry] brought from Egypt . . ." (Ezekiel 23:8). The Egyptians worshipped calves as well as other idols. Israel learned idolatry in Egypt, which represents a type of the world's system.

Today idolatry is a foreign word to the American Church. We don't consider the warnings God gave concerning idolatry as having any application to us. We have no golden statues or altars. Americans would never be involved in that. What we don't realize is Americans have set up more idols than can be numbered. The dictionary defines idolatry as "1) the worship of idols or 2) excessive adoration or reverence of any person or thing." They don't realize an idol is something given attention to before God. Because we don't envision idols accurately, American Christians are entangled by them as easily as the children of Israel.

To simplify the words of Paul, we are not to give our affections and love to the things the world gives its affections and love to, because we **cannot have a part in both the Lord's table and the table of demons.**

Remember God commanded, "You shall have no other gods **before** Me" (Exodus 20:3). An idol is what we put **before** God in our lives! Anything we like, trust, love, adore, desire, worship, hope in, have faith in, give our attention to, and seek more than the Lord.

In 1983 I left a very good-paying engineering job with Rockwell International to enter the ministry of helps full-time. I took a several thousand dollar a year pay cut. I made a sacrifice that made it look like I was totally sold out to Jesus without any desires of my own.

In 1986 I went to the Philippines with another minister. I thought God was sending me over there to preach. I didn't realize God was really sending me to change my life forever! The second night of the meetings, the other minister preached a message on the Lordship of Jesus Christ. He began to show how Jesus must be received as Lord not just as savior! He shared how the word "Lord" appears over seventy-eight hundred times in the Bible and "Savior" only thirty-seven! I sat in service under deep conviction. Here I was a minister and had never heard anything like this in all my life! I took a look at my life. Was Jesus Christ really supreme in authority? Or was I giving only lip service to Him by calling Him Lord? Was He really on the throne of my life, or did **I worship the Lord, and serve my own gods (idols), after the manner of our nation . . . ?**"

I returned home, and within a few days I placed a chair in the center of a large room, saying, "God, this chair represents the throne of my heart. I am not leaving this room until Jesus Christ is there to stay." I was tired of saying He was Lord without Lordship over every area of my life. Often we only let Jesus rule in the areas in which we want His rule. *Jesus Christ* needs to be *Lord of all of your life!* For two hours I circled that chair. Many things came to me as I prayed. I had far too much control over my own life, even in the full-time ministry. There was a tremendous struggle because my soul did not want to give up its lordship! I began to weep, yet my heart was set. No matter what He desired of me, I would follow!

Now began the exposure of these idols! First came professional sports, a big part of enjoyment in my life. I was an avid fan of the Dallas Cowboys. Every Sunday after service I'd sit and watch them play. If my wife needed help, forget it, "Honey, the Cowboys are playing." We'd eat at half-time or after the game. I was a good Christian man who did not smoke, drink, lie, or commit adultery. But God was about to expose an idol!

One Sunday as I was watching a very exciting ball game, the Spirit of God came on me to pray! There was a tremendous burden, and I knew it meant *now*. But I said, "Lord, there are only eight minutes left in the game. Please wait. I'll pray for five hours when this game is over." Waiting eight more minutes wouldn't hurt. I thought, "I'll give him five hours or more if He needs me after the game." I thought I was being very generous! The only problem was the burden didn't lift, even after my generous offer. So, know what I did? I watched the rest of the game, then went to my prayer closet to pray, and the enabling had lifted. The burden was gone! God did not want a sacrifice of five hours from me, He wanted obedience! Obedience is better than sacrifice. God wanted to know if He or the Cowboys were first. I knew then I had put the Cowboys before Him. I never would have said it, but my actions proved it. I had made the Dallas Cowboys an idol. I was in the full-time ministry and couldn't leave a ball game to obey God! Remember God says, "You shall not make idols for yourselves . . ." (Leviticus 26:1). Now, what may be an idol to one person is not necessarily an idol to another. **You** are the one who makes it an idol. I humbled myself and asked God for His grace to remove it from my heart. I began to tear down that idol by no longer giving it place. I stopped watching games, and the desire eventually was gone. Today I can watch the Cowboys play, and there is no attraction. As a matter of fact, it is now boring to me to watch professional football!

Golf was another idol in my life. I loved playing golf. I thought about it constantly. I would get up at 4:30 A.M. and go to the course to make a tee time for two days later. Yet to get up at 4:30 to pray was a different matter. It was a struggle to pray but a joy to play golf. One day I was out praying, and in the middle of prayer I was seeing the ninth hole of my favorite course in Dallas, wishing I could be out playing. The Lord spoke to me: "John, give your golf clubs to your friend Matt." I knew God had spoken, and I was trying to ignore it. I had just bought a brand new set of clubs and bag worth over $500. My previous set was stolen out of our garage, and insurance had covered the new set. I had only used the clubs once and loved them. I thought, "If I give these away, I won't be able to buy another set." It took four days for me to do, but on the fourth day my wife and I drove over to this friend's house and gave him the set of clubs. On the way over my wife said, "Honey, are you sure God told you?" But as soon as I gave them away I had joy and knew this sport no longer was an idol. I drew closer in fellowship to the Lord as a result of it.

A year later an amazing thing happened. A man came up to my wife and said, "Open up your trunk; I have something for your husband." He proceeded to throw in a set of clubs and a bag. We then moved to Florida, and within weeks another man said, "Open your trunk; I have something for you." He had been on the professional golf circuit and gave me the finest set of golf clubs, worth approximately $2,000. He looked at me and said, "God told me to give them to you. Golf is out of place in my life." At first I thought, "Is this is a trap of the enemy to bring me back into bondage?" However, God said, "Accept them, they are from Me."

Those clubs sat in my garage for a year and a half, and I only used them once. God had put it in place in my life. Today I play occasionally as a means of rest and fellowship. It is important for us to have "re-creation," times of rest and refreshing. They keep us sharp and focused. The game no longer is an idol to me. If God told me to give up the sport again, I would do it without hesitation because it no longer has a hold on me.

The third idol was food! You may ask, "How can food be an idol? It is a necessity of life." If it is a fulfillment in your life before God, it is an idol. I weighed only 150 pounds, but I loved eating. I would rather eat than do most anything. I'd eat even if I wasn't hungry. Then if I was too stuffed, I would look forward to just a slight return of hunger so I could indulge in more food. Many people are like this. They don't allow themselves to drink or smoke but give their flesh its craving through food. They are under a legalistic way of life. They abstain from drinking and smoking not out of love for God but because of "law." It is not against their religious law to indulge in food, so they are bound to socially acceptable excesses.

The process God used to expose this idol was similar to the way He exposed the Cowboys. One morning I was about to pour a bowl of my favorite cereal when the Spirit of God spoke: "John, I want you to fast breakfast this morning." I knew it was Him. My first thought was, "Boy am I hungry; I'm looking forward to this breakfast (it was my favorite meal at the time)." Next I began to reason, "Why is the Lord telling me to fast with only ten minutes to pray before I go to work? What can be accomplished in such a short amount of time? I know, I will fast next Monday, Tuesday, and Wednesday." I thought God would be pleased with my sacrifice, over obedience! So I poured my cereal and ate. God used this to show me food was an idol! He showed me I preferred it over obeying Him! This truth set me free from that bondage. Today eating has its proper place in my life. I still enjoy it, but when I am satisfied, I stop.

CAN BLESSINGS BE IDOLS?

Often idols are simply the everyday things of life. The same was true with the children of Israel. They took simple earrings of gold and formed a calf of gold. These earrings were provided by God when they spoiled the Egyptians. The Lord caused the Egyptians to give their articles of gold and silver to the children of Israel (Exodus 12:36).

Again, an idol is nothing in itself, it is what we make it

in our hearts. Their hearts were not after God, but what they wanted. As long as God moved powerfully and provided what they wanted, they worshipped Him. He split the Red Sea—they were jubilant with praises, dancing before the Lord. He buried their enemies—Miriam and *all* the women took the timbrel and danced, praising God. But in the absence of His miracle-working power, or of Moses, they revealed what was really in their hearts. Three days later, complaining began. How could they be so ungrateful, turning so quickly from trusting God? Easy: they had idols in their hearts and were not satisfied with God alone! God testified against Israel, "She has never given up her harlotry [idolatry] brought from Egypt . . ." (Ezekiel 23:8).

Moses was different. He pursued God no matter how difficult things got or how distant God seemed! He had one desire, to know God! Everything else in his life focused toward that goal.

If your desire is anything other than to know God intimately, it will show up in dry or trying times. The base of idolatry is self-seeking. The New Testament refers to it as "covetousness."

> Therefore put to death your members which are on the earth: fornication, uncleanness, passion, evil desire, and **covetousness, which is idolatry** (Colossians 3:5).

To covet means to **desire intensely**. This comes from a self-willed directed person, not from a person who has counted the costs and forsaken all to follow Jesus. God wants us to be blessed and enjoy the good things He has placed on this earth. However, if these things become more dear than Him, they are in danger of becoming idols.

I was out praying, and upon conclusion of a four-day fast, this prayer came forth from my heart, and my head heard it after I had already uttered it. "God, my Father, if the blessings You have given me ever replace my love for You, then remove them from my life!" My head kicked in and argued, "Wait a minute. He gave me those blessings. I shouldn't pray a prayer like that!" My heart was quick to respond that even the blessings of God can be turned into an idol. Don't seek the blessings and not the blesser! Remember how the children of Israel came into the promised land and quickly forgot God had blessed them with it, and began to erect idolatrous places of worship in the land! Second Kings 17:10 says, "They set up for themselves sacred pillars and wooden images on every high hill and under every green tree." Jeremiah cried out to Israel about taking their promises and turning them into idols:

> The LORD said also to me in the days of Josiah the king: "Have you seen what backsliding Israel has done? She has gone up on **every high mountain and under every green tree,** and there **played the harlot . . ."** So it came to pass, through her casual harlotry, that she defiled the land and **committed adultery with stones and trees** (Jeremiah 3:6-9).

In the book of Malachi, God addresses the priests of Israel:

> "And now, O priests, this command-

ment is for you. If you will not hear, and if
you will not take it to heart, to give glory
to My name," says the Lord of hosts, "I
will send a curse upon you, and **I will curse
your blessings. Yes, I have cursed them
already, because you do not take it to heart**"
(Malachi 2:1).

In the New Testament, Jesus multiplied two small fish
and five barley loaves to feed the multitudes, then went
to the other side of the sea. The next day the multitudes
came seeking Jesus. Instead of being flattered because
they had come all the way around the sea, searching for
Him, He rebuked them, knowing they sought Him
because He had filled their stomachs and not because
they recognized who He was! He had only been their
resource in a time of need! Many seek God in a crisis situation, but in times of peace, they turn back to their
idols for their joy, not to God!

As a father of three boys, I love and desire nice things
for them. Often I bring home presents from my trips. I
love watching their excited faces as they enjoy their gifts.
Can you imagine how I'd feel if all they saw me as was a
present giver, only giving me attention when I brought
presents? What if another man who was not their father
began to give them presents and their hearts turned
toward him because he gave them what they wanted? He
had not fathered them, taught, cared, nor corrected
them. But if their motive was what they could get from
me, their hearts would be easily won over. Can you now
see why God says He is a jealous God? He has Fathered
us, and He desires our love as dear children. He has
given so freely to us and desires the same from us.

Once, while I was out praying in the woods, preparing for a service, the Lord said, "John, ask My people if they would want Me to serve them as they have served Me? If they would want My faithfulness to be like theirs?" I melted with sorrow thinking how we have served Him. He has given Himself totally for us. We are told, "He is also able to save to the uttermost those who come to God through Him, since **He always lives** to make intercession for them" (Hebrews 7:25). Not only did He give Himself completely to us by dying for us, but even now He still gives Himself in intercession for us.

A HOLY BRIDE

God is sending a prophetic anointing "to make ready a people prepared for the Lord." Their words shall wash and purify the people of God, changing their hope or desire totally toward Him and not the idols the world pursues. In Ephesians 5:25-27 we see Christ gave Himself for the Church "that He might **sanctify** and **cleanse** her with the washing of water **by the word**, that He might present her to Himself **a glorious Church**, not having spot or wrinkle or any such thing, but that **she** should be holy and without blemish." Notice the Church is referred to as *she*. Paul is comparing the relationship of Christ and the Church as a man and his wife. The Church takes the role of the wife or bride in this portion of scripture. He reinforces this in verse 32: ". . . I speak concerning Christ and the church."

Now let me ask you this question: Imagine a woman promising the man she is engaged to, "Honey, I will be a great wife. I'll cook the finest meals, keep a clean house, and always look good. I will be faithful to you 364 days a

year. Just give me one day a year on which I can commit
adultery with my old boyfriends." Would you agree to
this? What if she said, just four hours a year? Would you
agree to that? What about ten minutes? Most would not
agree to any of these propositions. Who would marry a
person like that? Though she has offered to be a great
mom and cook, she has not given her whole heart. She
still has other lovers, even though she commits adultery
only once a year.

Can you imagine Jesus coming back for a bride with
the same attitude? With hearts given to idols? Now we
understand why Paul cries out to the New Testament
Church: **"Therefore, my beloved, flee from idolatry"** (1
Corinthians 10:14). And why John warns, **"Little children, keep yourselves from idols. Amen"** (1 John 5:21).

10 GOOD ROOT— GOOD FRUIT

It is a relationship, not a law.

"Therefore **bear fruits worthy of repentance** . . . and even now the ax is laid to the **root of the trees**. Therefore every tree which does not bear good fruit is cut down and thrown into the fire."   Luke 3:8

THE ROOT IS WHAT PRODUCES THE FRUIT

Many people, when they repent of sin, deal only with the fruit, not the root! If you pick fruit from a tree, it will grow back. But if you sever the root of a tree, the fruit never returns! In order to achieve this, we must repent of the motive of the heart that produces the fruit of sin. All sin is self-motivated. If one sins for another, it is still done for selfish reasons. Therefore, the root of all sin is selfishness. The love of God, on the other hand, seeks not its own (1 Corinthians 13:5). We are exhorted by the word of God to be *rooted* and grounded in love (Ephesians 3:17). If we walk in perfected love, we will not sin, just as a tree with good roots cannot produce bad fruit. God is not self-seeking! It is His very nature to give. He is love! In order to be rooted in God's love we must first understand His love for us.

A few years after I became a Christian, I was driving home from work, and the Lord said to me, "John, do you know I esteem you better than Myself!" I could not believe what I had heard Him say. How could He esteem me better than Himself? He was the One who created the heavens and earth. He is God! So I said to Him, "Lord, I cannot accept this unless You give me three scriptures out of the New Testament to confirm what You are saying to me." He did not rebuke me, because out of the mouth of two or three witnesses every word is established. So He said, "What does Philippians chapter 2 say?" I opened the Bible and read as follows:

> Let nothing be done through **selfish ambition** or conceit, but in lowliness of mind **let each esteem others better than himself** (Philippians 2:3).

The Lord said, "There is your first scripture." I responded, "Lord, You're speaking of Your relationship to me. Paul was writing the Philippian Christians and telling them to esteem each other better than themselves." He responded, "John, I don't ever tell My children to do anything I do not do Myself." That is why there are so many problems in Christian homes. The parents tell their children not to behave a certain way and yet do it themselves. We tell our children not to fight and then we fight ourselves. Then our actions speak louder than our words, and children grow up imitating what they see rather than what is taught. I still wasn't too sure about this so I said, "That is only one scripture. You still need to give me two more!"

He then said, **"John, who hung on the cross, Me or you?"** I melted when He said that. He said, "I hung on the cross bearing *your* sins, *your* sicknesses and diseases, *your* poverty, *your* judgment, because I *esteemed you better than myself!*" He never committed any sin. As a matter of fact, He did not even have to come to earth. He could have let us all go to the everlasting lake of fire with the devil and his angels (Matthew 25:41). He came not for Himself but for us! The following were the second and third scriptures:

> Who Himself bore **our sins** in His own body on the tree, that we, having died to sins, might live for righteousness—by whose stripes you were healed (1 Peter 2:24).

> Be kindly affectionate to one another with **brotherly love**, in honor giving **preference to one another** (Romans 12:10).

He said, "John, I am 'the first born of many brothers'" (Romans 8:29). I did not realize the depth of His love until then. I knew then, if only one person had been lost, He would have willingly come and done the same thing. This kind of love is the foundation of the kingdom of God. It is what we are to be rooted in and how we are to treat each other!

SERVE OR BE SERVED

Because of rejection many do not understand this kind of love. Often children have been painfully rejected by their own parents. The way we view our earthly father affects the way we see our heavenly one. So God reveals Himself to us otherwise! The Elijah anointing is being sent to ". . . turn the hearts of the fathers to the children, and the hearts of the children to their fathers, lest I come and strike the earth with a curse" (Malachi 4:6).

We began to lose our fathers as a nation in the 1940s and '50s, and it has progressively gotten worse. Selfishness began this rejection process. The demands of fathering cut into men's success-oriented lives. Others were too lazy. Now many people see God as a taker, not a giver. They cannot receive His love for them because they feel it must be earned by winning His approval and love as they did with their earthly fathers.

Many fathers and leaders in the church are more concerned with their goals than with their children or people with whom God has entrusted them. People are only a resource to fulfill their vision. The success of their vision outweighs the purpose of it, leaving us without any disciples. Instead of serving the people God entrusts them with, they now demand to be served, which serves the vision.

After the last supper Jesus rose, took a towel, poured water into a basin, and began to wash the disciples' feet, drying them with the towel. He then said:

> Do you know what I have done to you? You call me Teacher and Lord, and you say well, for so I am. If I then, your Lord and Teacher, have washed your feet, you also ought to wash one another's feet. For I have given you **an example**, that you should do as I have done to you (John 13:12-15).

This is the leadership He has called us to. Leaders

who seek to serve, not to be served. I want to make a point: Jesus washed Judas' feet as well! He continually reached out even to the one about to betray Him. He did not use His authority to protect His own life or ministry!

How many times have leaders cut off men and women under them because they were are suspicious of them? The truth is they are insecure in their calling. They are not perfect in love; they fear that what has been given to them might be stolen. This was found in Saul. When he thought David was going to win the heart of the people, he sought to cut David off. Saul's men served him out of fear. David's men served him out of love. They knew him as a man after God's heart, with genuine love for the men under him. That is why when David but uttered his desire to drink from the well of Bethlehem, three men risked their lives, breaking through enemy lines to give him his desire. What was it about this man that would cause these men to do this? His care for them could be seen when they brought the water to him. He refused to drink it, for these men had put their lives in jeopardy for his own desire. Saul demanded respect while David earned the respect of his men.

Jesus gave us this mind-boggling command after washing the feet of His disciples. He says:

> "A new commandment I give to you, that you love one another; **as I have loved you,** that you also love one another. By this all will know that you are My disciples, if you have love for one another" (John 13:34-35).

Jesus commands, not suggests, that we love each other with the same love I just described! Esteeming each other better than ourselves. If we would be rooted in this kind of selfless love, sin would bear no more fruit! We would walk free from selfish motives. He said by this kind of love the world would recognize us as true disciples. They will not know it by what we preach! The world is tired of simply hearing that God changes lives; they want to see His life-changing power in Christians! It is not by the miracles done in His name that they will know us as His disciples. The Bible speaks of lying signs and wonders in the last days (2 Thessalonians 2:9). Miracles will get the attention, but the love of God will keep them. I have also heard preachers say the world will know we are His by our wealth in finances. We have certainly seen that is not true! The world today is mocking Christians because of their excessive love for gain! They see competition, jealousy, and haughtiness among Christians—hidden by the mask of ministry or Bible promises, but still motivated by the love of self!

IF YOU LOVE ME

How can we possibly keep this command of loving as He loves? How can we walk in that kind of love? If it is a command from God, that means it is not impossible. It is only impossible when we attempt it in our own strength. God would be unjust to give us a command that was impossible. Look closely at these words of Jesus:

"If you love Me, keep My commandments" (John 14:15).

I was preparing to minister, and the Spirit of God led me to this scripture. The way I saw it was God saying, "John, if you love Me, you will prove it by keeping My commandments." After I meditated on this a few moments, the Lord told me to read the scripture again. So I read it again. He said, "You did not get what I was saying—read it again." This went on till I read the scripture approximately ten times. Finally, I said, "Lord, forgive my ignorance; show me what You're saying!" He said, "John, I wasn't saying if you keep My commandments, you will prove you love Me. I already know whether you love Me or not! What I was saying was, if a man falls head over heels in love with Me, he will be enabled to keep My commandments!"

It is a relationship, not a law. The way I viewed it was law. Many today know Him this way. Instead of a love relationship with Him, they have substituted the seven steps to healing, four-point plan of salvation, five scriptures on prosperity, and the baptism of the Holy Spirit. They imagine God is somehow contained in their box of promises, to be pulled and claimed as they feel necessary. Then they wonder why they have so much trouble with sin! Why are His commandments so hard to keep? It is because they are not rooted in the love of God!

Let's illustrate this. Have you ever fallen in love? When I was engaged to my wife, Lisa, I was head over heels in love with her. I thought of her constantly. I'd do whatever was necessary to spend as much time with her as possible. If she needed something, no matter what I was doing or what time it was, I would jump in my car and get it for her. I didn't have to force myself to talk to people about her—I extolled her praises to anyone who would listen.

Because of my intense love for her, it was a joy for me to do whatever she wished. I didn't do these things to prove I loved her; I did them because I loved her. She had all my attention. My affections were set on her. I wasn't interested in any old girlfriends anymore. There was no other girl I wanted. She was the apple of my eye.

But a few short years into our marriage, I turned my attention and affection to other things, such as the work of the ministry. It was now bothersome to do something for her. Taken for granted, Lisa was not in my thoughts as much. Gifts for her came out of obligation on Christmas, anniversaries, and birthdays—and even that was a bother. Our marriage was in trouble. Our first love was dying! Because the intensity of our original love was no longer there, it was difficult even to get along. Since then God turned my heart and let me see how selfish I had become. Graciously, He rekindled the flames of our first love and healed our marriage. In light of this, you can understand why Jesus said:

> "Nevertheless I have this against you, that you have **left your first love.** Remember therefore from where you have fallen; **repent and do the first works,** or else I will come to you quickly and remove your lampstand from its place—unless you **repent**" (Revelation 2:4-5).

Jesus is speaking to the Church here! What does He mean, "repent and do the first works"? At the beginning of this address He says, "I know your works, your labor, your patience, and that you cannot bear those who are evil." So we are not talking about an inactive people. So why does He say, "Repent and do the first works." The answer is they were now serving Him out of obligation, not out of a love relationship. He is saying, Repent—change your heart, let your love return to Me; put away your idols and serve Me once again out of love, not tradition!

If our heart is rooted in intense love for Him, then keeping His commandments is not burdensome but a delight! How do we fall in love with Him and stay in love with Him? The answer is in the following scriptures:

> If ye then be risen with Christ, **seek** those things which are above, where Christ sitteth on the right hand of God. **Set your affection** on things above, not on things on the earth. . . . **Mortify therefore your members which are upon the earth;** fornication, uncleanness, inordinate affection, evil concupiscence, and covetousness, which is idolatry (Colossians 3:1-5).

What you seek is what your affections will be set on! If you seek success, your affections will be set on success—even if it is ministry! I thought constantly of Lisa during our engagement, how I could spend more time with her. I wanted to spend as much time as possible in her presence. When we seek the presence of God, our affections are set on Him. Many deceived Christians go to church, pay tithes, sing praise and worship songs, nod in agreement with the minister's message, and possibly help in the ministry, but it is all done out of obligation. However, if someone touches on an area where their affections are set, such as the upcoming Monday football game, they perk up with a sparkle in their eyes and with great excitement discuss who they think will win and why. Where are their affections *set*? What your affections are *set* on will dominate your thinking. I had no problems thinking about Lisa whenever work did not demand my full attention. Whenever I had a break from total concentration at work, my mind snapped back to where it was *set*—Lisa! When I first started watching the Dallas Cowboys, they held very little of my attention. However, that little attention began to grow the more I watched, talked, and thought about them, until they became an idol in my life. Conversely, the more you seek the Lord's presence, the more He'll manifest Himself to you, the more you will want to seek Him until the desire consumes you! Jesus showed this in John 14 a few verses later:

> He who has My commandments and keeps them, it is he who loves Me. And **he who loves Me** [the person who is seeking Him with all his heart] will be loved by My Father, and I will love him and **manifest Myself to him** (John 14:21).

The more we experience His manifested presence, the more we will want it. Where many fall short is their failure to keep seeking even when He does not seem to be near. God says in Jeremiah 29:13, "And you will seek Me and find Me, when you **search for Me with all your heart**." The key is searching for Him with *all your heart!* If you misplaced something of great value, you wouldn't look for it for five minutes and quit. You would search until you found it, no matter how long it took! Hebrews 11:6 says, "He is a rewarder of those who **diligently seek Him**." We must seek until we find—because He has promised us that if we diligently seek Him, we *will* find Him. It may not be in our time table, but we will find His presence!

Notice Colossians 3:5 says, "Mortify therefore your members which are upon the earth . . . ." Sin is put to death not by the law of works but by intensely seeking for Him. When we intensely seek for Him, our affections or love will be set on Him, thus putting to death the desires of the flesh! It goes back to what Jesus says, that if you fall head over heels in love with Me, you will delight in keeping my commandments. Too many are trying to crucify the deeds of the flesh without an active relationship with Him! Now you can understand what Paul meant in Galatians 5:16 when he said, "Walk in the Spirit, and you shall not fulfill the lust of the flesh." Being in the Spirit puts to death the desires of the flesh!

This is God's purpose for creating us! If you look at Adam in the garden of Eden, you see the reason for creation. God didn't put Adam in the garden to have a successful healing ministry, or a successful evangelistic ministry, or to cast out devils, or to have a large church. God created Him because He desired fellowship with him. The same is true today. God desires our fellowship. He is seeking those who will spend time with Him, not in religious prayers, but in spirit and truth.

Can you imagine me approaching my wife for intimacy with a outlined card in front of me. Step one: Tell her she is beautiful. Step two: Hold her hand. Step three: Look into her eyes and say, "I love you," etc. How far do you think I would get? Yet this is the relationship people eventually reduce theirs to with the Lord. If they continue in this legalistic pattern, they will feel their life ebb away. We should seek Him not out of obligation but because we desire His presence. We should communicate from our heart. We should hate sin because we love God and want nothing between us.

To take the example of my wife and me one step further, let's suppose I set up our time together for fellowship every day from 5-6 P.M. Anything she had to say would have to wait until 5 P.M. Then to make matters worse, at 5 P.M., I did all the talking for the entire hour.

She could not get a word in edgewise because I talked
nonstop. Then at 6 P.M. sharp, I got up, said it was wonderful, and left. What kind of relationship is that?

The example I just gave is like the rut I fell into a few
years back. I prayed for two hours every morning from
5-7. I would go outside and walk on a deserted road and
talk diligently to the Lord. I had my list to go over, as
well as whatever else came to my mind, as I prayed. I was
very proud of my diligence. Then one morning, upon
completion of my two-hour prayer time, I began the
walk home, and the Lord shook me, saying loudly in my
spirit, "I WOULD LIKE THE OTHER TWENTY-
TWO HOURS OF THE DAY!" He went on, "John,
you come out here almost every morning and pray for
two hours, and when you say 'Amen' at 7 A.M. you then
go about your activities of the day and shut Me out of
most of it." He showed me He wanted my heart open to
His voice at all times, not just during prayer. This is a
relationship of fellowship with God. Some of the greatest things God has revealed have come to me not in my
dedicated morning time but while driving the car, taking
a shower, mowing the lawn, or doing some other activity.
The Spirit of the Lord is with us every moment, not just
in our dedicated times of prayer. Don't misunderstand,
we should all have time daily when we can shut ourselves
in the closet of prayer and seek the Lord. But it should
be done out of desire to fellowship. Then when we come
away the communion with Him continues!

So many are caught in a spiritual rut of routine. They
may speak in tongues, sing songs of praise and worship,
and pray long prayers without any communion with the
Holy Spirit. Then they wonder why the fire is gone?
Why has serving God become dull? Why do attractions
of this life grab my attention easier than the things of

God? The answer: you have strayed from your purpose for creation—fellowship with the living God.

Jesus said to repent and do the first works. Serve Him out of a fiery love, not out of obligation. If love for Him is your root motive, then you will have the fruit of repentance. The fruit may or may not manifest immediately, but it will manifest. Therefore the work of repentance is not complete until fruit is manifested. Don't allow resistance of any type to stop you from knowing Him, but press on to the goal of the high call of God in Christ Jesus, to know Him as He knows you! May God's grace and presence be with you in Christ Jesus our Lord.

Now to Him who is able to keep you from stumbling, and to present you faultless before the presence of His glory with exceeding joy, to God our Savior, Who alone is wise, be glory and majesty, dominion and power, both now and forever. Amen (Jude 24-25).

ON THE AUTHOR

JOHN P. BEVERE, JR.

John Bevere attended Purdue University, graduating in 1981 with a Bachelor of Science degree in Mechanical Engineering. While at Purdue, John played varsity tennis and was a member of a fraternity. It was while in this fraternity that John was born again in January 1979 and filled with the Spirit on June 3 of that same year.

John attended Word of Faith Bible and Leadership Institute in Dallas, Texas, in 1981 and 1982. He then worked as Executive Staff Assistant at Word of Faith World Outreach Center, from June 1983 through November 1987.

From November 1987 to December 1989, John was the Youth/College/Career Pastor at Orlando Christian Center under Benny Hinn. In January 1990, John resigned from staff to travel full-time. Presently John travels from coast to coast and border to border, preaching the message God has put in his heart. John's vision for this nation is to see revival and restoration come through the prophetic preaching of repentance, prayer, holiness, and spiritual warfare . . . joining arms with local pastors to pull down strongholds and turn the hearts of the people back to God.

John and his wife, Lisa, reside in the Orlando, Florida, area and have three young sons—Addison David, Austin Michael, and Joshua Alexander.

ANOTHER BOOK BY
John Bevere

VICTORY IN THE WILDERNESS

GOD!
Where Are You?

Is this the cry of your heart? Does it seem your spiritual progress in the Lord has come to a halt—or even regressed? You wonder if you have missed God or somehow displeased Him, but that is not the case . . . you've just arrived at the wilderness! Now, don't misunderstand the purpose of the wilderness. It is not God's rejection, but the season of His preparation in your life. God intends for you to have *Victory in the Wilderness*. Understanding this season is crucial to the successful completion of your journey. It is the road traveled by patriarchs and prophets in preparation for a fresh move of God.

> "John Bevere is a young man who has been taught of God in the wilderness, and it shows—in fervency, anointing, discipline, and dedication. His ministry has been an inspiration to me, as well as to the church I pastor, and I know this book will inspire you."
> –Ron Domina, Senior Pastor
> Bethel Full Gospel, Rochester, New York

170 pages, $7.00
(Bookstore and volume discounts available)

The following is only one of many testimonies we have received as a result of lives being touched by this book:

> Dear John & Lisa,
> Today my laundry, dishes and housework piled up and I didn't answer the phone. I have laughed, cried, repented, shouted "Hallelujah" and praised the Lord for answers to months of prayers. All this happened because I sat down with my coffee at 6:00 this morning, opened your book, and have been unable to put it down!
> –Linda C.; Antioch, TN

VIDEO CASSETTE MESSAGES
by John Bevere

Baptism of Fire
Pursuing God

AUDIO CASSETTE MESSAGES
by John Bevere

Pursue the High Call
Breaking through Resistance
Escaping Religious Ruts
The Wilderness
Why Is Revival Withheld?
Overcoming Offenses
Call to War
Joy in the Holy Ghost
Suffering—The Road to Perfection
Fresh Vision
The Double Portion Anointing
The Elijah Prophets
Birthing in the Spirit

Bookstore and volume discounts available

To receive our free newsletter and a complete list of available materials
from John Bevere Ministries, or for information on having John Bevere or
his wife, Lisa, minister to your church, conference, retreat, or any other
ministry group, please contact the ministry at the following address:

John Bevere Ministries
P.O. Box 2002
Apopka, Florida 32704-2002
(407) 889-9617

Feel free to include your prayer requests and comments when you write.